TOWARDS EXCELLENCE IN UNIVERSITY EDUCATION

TOWARDS EXCELLENCE IN UNIVERSITY EDUCATION

By

Prof. A.K. Jain

Eminent Citizen, MGNREGA (MORD)
Ex-Commissioner (Planning), DDA
New Delhi – 110 001
(India)

Foreword by

Dr. Ashok K. Chauhan

Founder President
Amity Group of Education

DISCOVERY PUBLISHING HOUSE PVT. LTD.
NEW DELHI-110 002

Published by:
Tilak Wasan
DISCOVERY PUBLISHING HOUSE PVT. LTD.
4383/4B, Ansari Road, Darya Ganj
New Delhi-110 002 (India)
Phone : +91-11-23279245, 23253475, 43596065
E-mail : discoverybooksindia@gmail.com
discoverypublishinghouse@gmail.com
namitwasan9@gmail.com
web : www.discoverypublishinggroup.com

***First Edition:* 2018**

ISBN: 978-93-5056-466-0

Towards Excellence in University Education

Printed at:
Infinity Imaging Systems
Delhi

Foreword

"A University is expected to be a place of higher learning where an individual is helped to acquire more knowledge, refine his or her culture and master philosophy. One should give up greed and selfishness and work hard with devotion...A University is not mere information shop, it is a place where one's intellect, will and emotions are disciplined. The university is a sanctuary of the intellectual life of the country, and pursuit of knowledge is the soul of the university".

Dr. Sarvapalli Radhakrishnan, Former President of India

According to the vedic wisdom *"learning is the greater personality of man; it is his hidden and safely deposited wealth; it is a teacher of teachers; it is a kinsman. Learning promotes an indescribable happiness of all times". (Bhartrahart, Satakas).*

The university education is undergoing a paradigm shift. Technical courses are connecting with the realms of ecology, economics, management and humanities and vice versa. This interdependence is breaking down the rigid boundaries and making education more humane, value based and relevant to cultural, environmental and social context. With a cross-disciplinary education, it is possible to respond to the breadth and depth of the complexities of development. It is necessary to equip younger generation to tackle innumerable social, cultural, economic and environmental issues, which our country is facing. The greatest enterprise of the mind has always been the manifestation of the linkages among thought, context and processes. The university education must endeavour developing a creative mindscape which facilitates the connectedness between the individual and overall excellence. This needs new skills, values and dedication.

Prof. A.K. Jain in his book talks about the idea of organizing the thoughts which is central to learning process. He gives an eight steps process which starts with cleaning, de-cluttering, emptying, opening locks and unlearning. The learner then proceeds to observe, listen, digest, assimilate and understand. He emphasises that learning is most likely to occur when people have participated actively in the process. He cites a UNICEF study, according to which 83 per cent of learning is by sight and we remember 50 percent when we see and hear and 90 per cent what we say and do. As such graphics and visuals together with inductive and experimental methods of learning are most useful in higher education. As it is said, each picture is equal to thousand words, the graphics can open up a new world of learning and communicating in a clear, simple way.

Prof. A.K. Jain refers to Edward de Bono's concept of lateral thinking. He explained that this is a five stage process: where we are going or the purpose of thinking, looking into the information, generating alternative ideas, selection of the best alternative and finally actioning. The hall mark of lateral, thinking is innovation by a blend of theory, technology and performance. Too much focus on formal, curriculum based teaching marginalizes the creative abilities. A creative mind can be developed by soft mediums which are metaphorical, humourous and playful. We have heard of Panchtantra fables, which transformed the incorrigible, most unwilling princes into creative and wise young men. The masters stand apart because of their soft, innovative and lateral thinking. Soft methods educate the student by triggering his own thinking and search for connections among things. Every Indian has a background of soft thinking-mythology, metaphors, visual, graphics, poetry, play, etc. which can be cross-breaded with hard mediums of teaching and learning. As told by Ramana Maharishi, *"a student has to be like an empty cup to fill it up. The grace of guru is like an ocean. If one come with a cup he will only get a cupful. It is no use complaining of the niggardliness of the ocean.*

The bigger the vessel the more one will be able to carry. It is entirely upto the student".

During my 28 years of continuous stay in West Germany (now Germany) and reaching to the great heights in my professional career, being regarded as most successful non-German born entrepreneur in the country, I got the urge to study and know more about the most successful people in the European continent and also in the United States of America. I came to the conclusion that it is the Education only which acts as a jumping board and leads the persons to such high success. I then became more curious to learn about the education system in various top universities, Wharton, Harvard, MIT, Stanford, Cornell, Yale, Carnegie Mellon from USA and Oxford, Cambridge, London School of Economics, University College, London in UK, just to name the few which I visited, held lectures there, interacted with the students and the faculty and tried to understand not only their curriculum, but most importantly about the teaching style and methodologies of their professors. I came to the insight that it is the teaching style and the methodology of the teacher which makes a student attentive, dedicated, and interested.

There and then, I got the obsession that in view of the great human resource in India and having an ideal demographic divide, having 65% of the population below the age of 35 and 44% of the population under the age of 14 years, I started the Amity Group of Education with the single point aim and mission that why should not our universities from India rank among the top universities globally. To attain this, I used to sit in the classes of experienced renowned professors at Amity University and among them was also Prof. A.K. Jain whose teaching style and methodology greatly influenced me. I sat with him many times and exchanged views with him, took his advice as to how Amity University can be made a university with best practices and ideal governance. For this, teaching was seen as a pivotal factor. Having belief in this idea, the next step was to galvanize the concept into practice. My vision has been that besides excellence in education, it should also develop a pluralistic diversity with spiritual, mental and physical growth of the student, the students those who are committed to the human values, freedom, autonomy, inclusion and academic excellence.

When the manuscript of the book of Prof. A.K Jain came in my hand with the request to write a Foreword, I found that this book is going to be the ideal book which would transform the lives of the students, who in turn would make India within a short span of time, a Knowledge Superpower and in times to come, a global superpower. I am convinced that this book would give to a large number of teaching faculty fraternity to think on their ways and means, as to how do they teach and would make them not only a better teacher but an ideal teacher, which would lead to a revolutionary and mighty force to contribute for the nation building.

We have long way to go. We always remember that university education is the most important segment of nation building and its future. As such, we have to give our best to the society and nation, not just for the present, but for posterity. While gratified by the fulfilled vision of making one of the most remarkable contribution to higher learning, I always remember the words of Robert Frost *"The woods are lovely, dark and deep, But I have promises to keep, And miles to go before I sleep, and miles to go before I sleep"*.

I would recommend the students and the esteemed faculty to read what Prof. A.K. Jain says about achieving Excellence in University Education. I am confident that this book would make a very pleasant and enriching reading, as the author has sprinkled food for thought with interesting and tasty quotes, visuals, graphics and humour.

It gives me great pleasure to write Foreword for this unique book of Prof. A.K Jain which would be regarded as one of the best books in the area of education and I compliment and appreciate the writer for such highly praiseworthy efforts.

Dr. Ashok K. Chauhan
Founder President
Amity Group of Education

Preface

India has landed right at the bottom of the survey of higher educational quality across 50 major nations conducted by Universitas 21, an international network of leading research-intensive universities.

—*Times of India, 14th June 2012*

Being a visiting faculty in Management/Planning courses, I observed that very few students were actually learning. On an average out of 30 students 6 to 8 were occupied with the mobile phones, 4 to 6 students were busy with their laptops, and 6 to 8 students talking among themselves, besides 4 to 6 students usually missing. At the end of two hour lecture, I would ask a simple question and take the debriefing where only 3 students that is merely 10% seemed to absorb something. The general reaction of my colleagues in the faculty was that there was a lack of discipline and interest among the students, too many diversions and distractions, changing values and poor educational background. However, I was keen to hear from the horse's mouth. 60 to 70 per cent students found the lectures boring, complicated, overloaded, difficult, punishing and even intimidating.

This made me to think and change my teaching style so as to make the subject absorbing and interesting and making the students more involved. They were motivated to attend the class for something interesting and new and not just for the sake of minimum attendance. This made me to realize the importance of simplifying the ways of explaining the difficult and complicated topics (without hiding the complexity of the simple). The students were put in focus, not the teacher and his intellectual excellence. Anecdote style, a dash of humour and a consistent story-line with clarity and simplicity, did the magic. The metaphors, graphics, matrix charts and case studies helped to simplify the complex, generating interest among the students. Group exercises were given to the students where the faculty acts as a friendly guide and facilitator. The teacher climbs down from the high pedestal of 'guru' and mixes up with the students giving them personal touch and attention. At the end, students have the pride of achievement and creative work. The group discussions kept every student awake and involved. As a result take away of learning increased to as much as 80 to 90 per cent that is 10 times the conventional learning. It means value addition for time and money. It implies less is more and a win-win for both - the students and teacher. This is how in some world class institutes almost every graduate turns out a useful resource for his employer and for the society. They are the best advertisements and testimonials for their alma mater.

This book is about learning that makes the students always striving towards citius, altius and fortius *i.e.*, faster, higher and stronger. In fact every teacher is a learner. I have been learning and practising since last four decades. I am struck by the enthusiasm of the younger generation who want to change the world. They are bubbling with energy and ideas and dismantling the walls between the teacher and learner. As a learner, I benefited much from the School of Public Policy, University of Birmingham; IHS, Erasmus University, Rotterdam; Illinois Institute of Technology, Chicago; Delhi School of Planning and Architecture; Amity University; Jindal Global Business School and University of Petroleum and Energy Studies.

During past decade professional education in India witnessed a quantum leap and a paradigm shift by way of privatisation. The pioneer and a visionary who stands out among many educationist-entrepreneurs is Dr. Ashok K. Chauhan, who has written an inspiring foreword for this book.

A publisher is akin to a lamp who spreads knowledge. Mr. Tilak Wasan of Discovery Publishing House (P) Ltd. is not only aware of this, but has a passion for producing quality books - both in content and presentation. I am fortunate that he readily accepted my request to publish this book.

A.K. Jain

Contents

Foreword by Dr. Ashok K. Chauhan

Preface

1. **Professional Education in India** 1

Islands of Individual Excellence—Education and Industry Interface—Lifelong Learning Striving Towards Citius (faster) Altius (higher) and Fortius (Stronger)—Rethinking Skill Development—Learning Curve—Changing Roles.

2. **The Idea of Learning** 13

Cleansing, Decluttering and Unlearning—Meditation—Focus—Multiview—Listening and Learning—Rigour, Persistence—Values—Active Learning—Soft and Hard Mediums.

3. **Participatory Learning** 41

Participatory Learning—Group Behaviour—Content versus Process—Communication—Decision-Making Procedure—Behaviours Relevant to the Group Learning—Emotional Issues—Individual Characteristics—Innovator—Resource Investigator—Chair—Shaper—Evaluator—Team Worker—Organiser—Finisher.

4. **World Class Education** 56

Improvised Performance—Mastering a Skill—The Myth of Talent and Luck—Embedded Learning—New Generation—Technology Platforms and Open ended Learning (OELE)—Social Learning—Lateral Thinking.

5. Personal Organisation 73
Education or Learning?
6. Communicating Effectively 78
Graphic Tools.
References 107
Index 109

CHAPTER 1

Professional Education in India

> ***A man is but a product of his thoughts what he thinks, he becomes.***
>
> —*Mahatma Gandhi*

The higher professional and technical education in India is fast growing. With more than 8000 institutes in degree sector, 2500 in the polytechnic sector, and more than 1.5 million seats at the entry level in the degree stream, 0.5 million in the polytechnic stream, we have one of the largest technical education sysems in the world. Today, a student who wishes to get into a technical education programme can do so. The problems like finding the finances are facilitated through educational loans from the banks.

According to the Ministry of Human Resource Development (MHRD) by 2022, India aims to have 500 million skilled people. For a country which, as World Bank says, has only 25 per cent of its graduates employment-ready, it is a worrisome scenario. While countries like Australia, Germany, South Korea have robust systems of skills development and vocational training, India has yet to wake up in terms of the skills deficit. It is time to tackle with astute policy decisions and effective implementation, to avoid demographic dividend.

Policy papers from MHRD, University Grants Commission (UGC) and All India Council for Technical Education (AICTE) do discuss skills development, but we have a long way to go before we integrate it into the core practices of mainstream education and relevant to the actual operations. Training for soft skills needs innovative methodologies, sophisticated blend of advanced technological equipments and creativity of human mind infrastructure and a vision of collective excellence.

There is tremendous pressure on the system to respond to the new expectations like finding suitable teaching faculty in all these Institutes, retaining them over long periods of time, providing them a facilitating mechanism to grow amongst their peers, an enabling mechanism to prosper in the societal expectations, and a suitable placement for almost 1.5 million youngsters graduating from our Universities every year. It would be worthwhile to note that a student with 50 per cent minimum eligibility at the qualifying examination also gets into this sytem along with the student at the top of the ladder. A teacher's role assumes tremendous significance in this context. Unfortunately, a normalisation of the process caters to common denominator and hence a fall in standard. The examination systems, being what they are, cater to a common denominator, that aid in propagating mediocrity. A university professor once set an examination question in which he asked "what is the difference between ignorance and apathy". The professor had to give an A+ to a student who answered. "I don't know and don't care."

For a country which requires to train and upskill 500 million people by 2022, skills development is an integral part of the education policy. Unfortunately, Indian education system has fallen short of this and we are starting a contradiction - millions of educated youths and manpower crunch of skilled knowledge professionals. While education imparts one kind of training to them, industry and markets are looking for another kind of skills set. There is an obvious disconnect between eudcation imparted to the youth and the market requirement and demand. To add to this, there are newer, emerging areas in which new skills are required for which India has yet to apply itself. The result is that the degree holders are seeking jobs, there is a manpower crunch, but still they are being denied the jobs being not useful to employer. Skills development needs to link up with the education, employment and resources. To upskill its youth, the conventional education framework needs to be revisited. Government alone cannot accomplish this task. It will call for a concerted effort of the government, private players and NGOs to address the issue in a comprehensive manner. If India is to gain its rightful place in the world, reap equal benefits and opportunities for all and rise from the debris of poverty and several other pressing issues, skills development will require to be given priority.

As per an estimate (FICCI, Ernst & Young report, 2010) the higher education expenditure is going to increase Rs. 1,55,015 crores and requires an investment of Rs. 360,640 crores ($ 76 bn) by 2020 to create the additional capacity. The amount accounts for around 1.9 per cent of the current GDP based on Purchasing Power Parity. Realizing the need to increase the public spend on higher education from a mere 0.7 per cent of GDP in the Eleventh Plan, the government is proposing to raise it to 1 per cent of the GDP during the Twelfth Plan. That would still leave a deficit which needs increased private sector investment.

Private, public and governmental participation and investments have been steadily increasing in the education sector. Forecasts suggests that, if current patterns of participation continue, more than 30 per cent of today's school leavers will experience higher education in 10 years from now. The present GER of about 15 per cent being pushed to 30 per cent, will mean better and more facilities of higher learning.

According to Prof. S.S. Mantha, Chairman of the All India Council for Technical Education (AICTE), the foremost three aspects of education are:

- The student,
- The faculty, and
- The institution.

If there were a way to plot these three properties individually and then have a map that plots all the institutes on a single page; it shall enable us to develop a credible system of rating, drawing up a median and then identifying need-gaps in colleges that remain below the median will help us improve the performance of the colleges and reduce the base area of the education pyramid. Indeed there are underlying layers that form the crux of each of the above aspects:

- **the student:** financial, regional and aspirational mapping.
- **the faculty:** financial, regional, innovational and aspirational mapping.
- **the institution:** Its ability to create impact in its local vicinity, national and global realms, promote research, retain faculty and consistently out-perform its outturn each year.

Investigations have revealed that many faculty members are experiencing dissatisfaction in their work environments and are typically becoming more dissatisfied over time. A longitudinal study by Sorcinelli (1994), for example, found 33 per cent of new faculty in their first year reported being very stressed. This percentage rose to 49 per cent in year two, and went to 71 per cent in year five.

A new Ph.D. faculty or someone who has worked in industry and joins a university, is faced with balancing many different issues. The faculty member must learn the procedures at the institution, university, teach, examine the students and get involved in research programmes. This is a challenge. Orientation programmes help but only so. In this scenario, there are several missing links which need to be plugged:

- Too much focus on individual excellence that marginalizes the students and the institutional competence.
- Overvaluing intellectualism and personal credentrials (doctor, persons, etc.) that make teaching too overloaded and complex for the tender minds of young students.
- Research for the sake of the research, divorced from its application and real life.

- Gaps between academic idealism and business process and procedures.
- Business like advertisements with emphasis on 'world class' education forgetting the local reality and constraints.
- After the privatisation of higher education, there is cut-throat competition among the institutes who aspire to become the islands of individual excellence, ignoring the principle of synergy and networking.

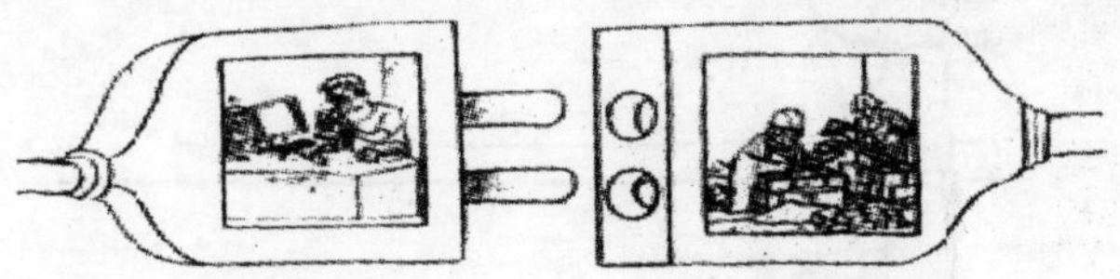

Connecting the Missing Links

Individual Excellence	↔	Institutional Competence
Intellectualism	↔	Common Concerns/Issues
Research	↔	Application
Academic Idealism	↔	Business Processes & Practices
Global Image	↔	Local Reality

Islands of Individual Excellence : An institute of excellence is a think tank which integrates learning, academics and research with the field and industry.

Graph of Professional's Image and Money

"Man, proud Man, dressed in a little brief authority, most ignorant of what he is most assured, his glassy essence like an angry ape, plays such tricks before high heaven, as to make the angels weep."

—William Shakespeare

Research and Applicaton Disconnect

Education and Industry Interface

In order to bring the gap between learning and practice, as well as to equip the students to play a vital role in the socio-economic development process, the following reforms are necessary in the higher/professional education:

- Orientation towards new methods of teaching and learning.
- Formal interface and exchange of education as research with industry, government and practice.
- In-service traning and QIP.
- Faculty Orientation and field experience/exchange.

The reforms in education and curriculum have to be derived from the review of 'process' and **Education – Industry Interface.** The 'process' essentially involves the following:

- Reassessment of the needs of higher education
- Reassessing the levels of professional education
- Thrust Areas
- Practical Learning

The Education-Industry Interface comprises the following critical areas :

- Practical training/internship
- Quality Focus
- Curriculum Reforms
- Career Prospects

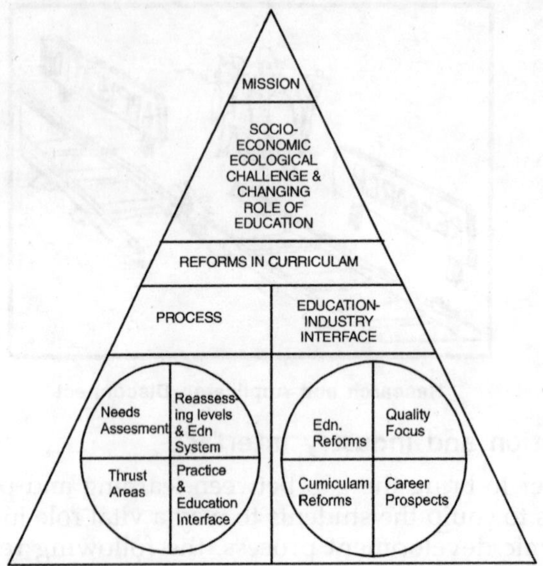

The Pyramid of Process and Education Reforms

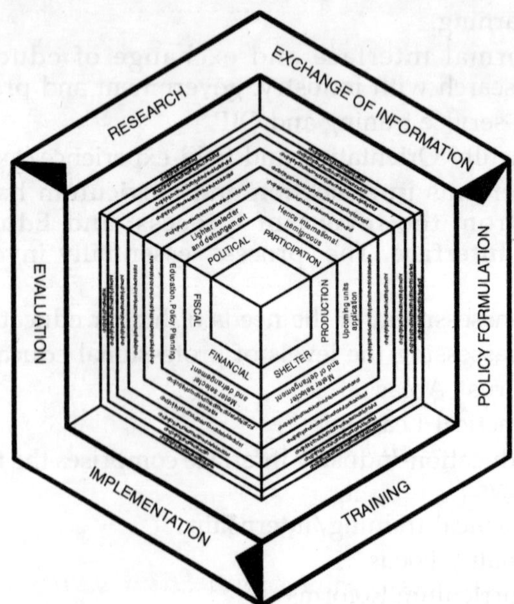

The Cycle of Learning and Research

The Sun of Lifelong Learning that Dispels the Clouds of Ignorance

Lifelong learning involves the integration of Basic skills, Professional skills of Organizational/Management Skills, and a synthesis of various pertinent aspects, that is Institutional/Organisational, Human, Political, Socio-cultural, Sustainability/Environmental and Operational/Implementation aspects of development. The sun of lifelong learning rises from the stages of courage, confidence, consciousness, conscience and creativity, which a student has to inculcate.

Rethinking Learning and Skill Development

The process of learning starts with acquisition and radiation of Basic/Core learning. It builds up into professional learning that leads to various specialisations. Learning Encompasses:

(*i*) Knowledge

(*ii*) Reflection and Observation

(*iii*) Conceptualisation

(*iv*) Action

The skills necessary to be developed in each category can be as given below:

Table 1.1 : Skills Development - Examples of Critical Areas

Learning	Skill Development
Knolwedge	**Knowledge—Knowing the 'Unknown'** • Information System - Dev. and application • Procedures • Basic Theroy/Principles • History/heritage
Reflection and Observation	**From Knowledge to Comprehension Interpretation and Understanding** • Analysis • Value System • Interface with Env., Tech., Legal, Instt., Social and Financial Aspects • Understanding
Concept	**Conceptualising and integrating the Abstract ideas and Simplifying the complex** • Vision • Concept Development, Plant/Design • Presentation
Action	**From overview to details; from 'General' to Specific; from Thinking to Acting, Reacting and Interacting** • Management and Orgn. • Institutional Frame • Implementation • Management of Env., Tech., Legal, Social, Financing, Monitoring/Feedback • Interacting Skills

The objective of learning is to equip the student to take up adequately and effectively the responsibility of socio-economic and business development. As such the structure of education comprises three levels - core learning/mono-disciplines focus (Diploma), Professional/Multi-interdisci-plinary focus (graduate) and Research Specialised learning (P.G. Masters, Ph.D., QIP, Trag.) The education to be a mission oriented and demand-driven activity.

Mission: To Educate Professionals and Enable them to take up Adequately and Effectively the Responsibility of Development and Change Management

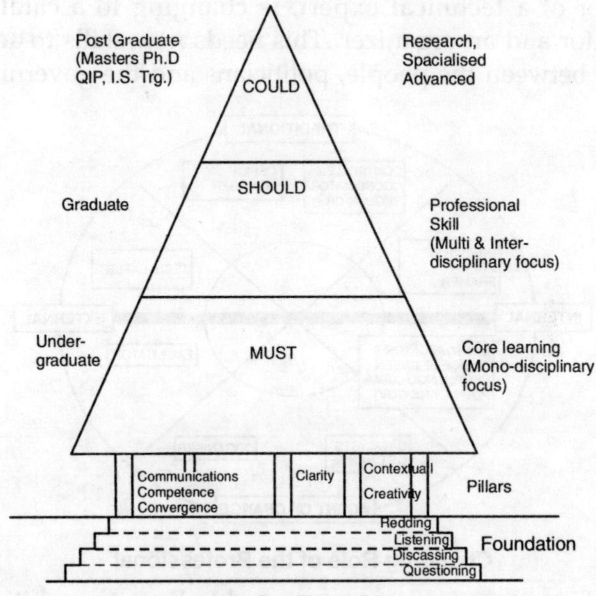

Learning Pyramid

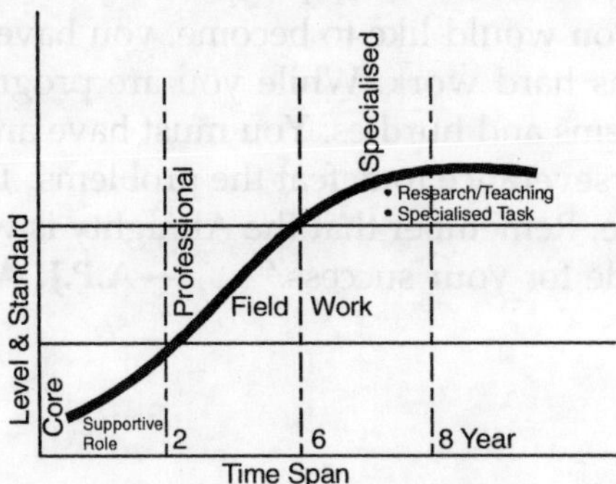

Learning Curve : The Learning Curve indicates the pace of learning which gradually builds up from core level to professional level. At specialised level, the pace of learning may be even quicker. However, being specialised, it may not necessarily raise the level of performance, or may not be effectively utilised where core and professional knowledge is required in day-to-day work.

Changing Roles

In the context of new challenges and changes in policy context, the traditional role of a professional, that of a manager, policy planner of a technical expert, is changing to a catalyst, a facilitator and an organizer. This needs new skills to act as a bridge between the people, politicians and the government.

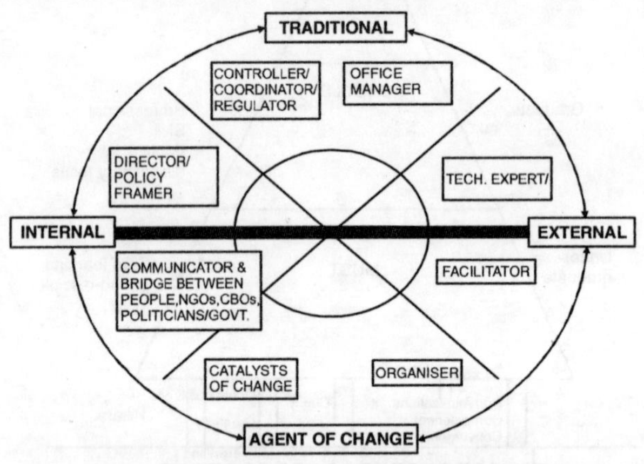

Changing Role of the Professional

"When you are young, you need to have an ambition for life. Think big and continuously acquire knowledge. Once you know what you would like to become, you have to sweat for it. That means hard work. While you are progressing, there will be problems and hurdles. You must have an indomitable spirit and perseverance to defeat the problems. Then you will succeed in life. Remember that the Almighty is with you, and he will collude for your success." —**A.P.J. Abdul Kalam**

CHAPTER 2

The Idea of Learning

> Take up one idea. Make that one idea of your life-think of it, dream of it, live on idea. Let the brain, muscles, nerves, every part of your body be full of that idea and just let every other idea alone. This is the way to success.
>
> —**Swami Vivekananda**

The path of realization of success by learning is akin to the game of ladders and snakes. It is a tough journey. Perceiving what is a ladder and what is a snake is a prerequisite. For a young student out of school, the university is a new world, new independence. In the midst of new friends, challenges and opportunities, he/she tastes new fashion and foods and is exposed to various kinds of entertainments that marginalize

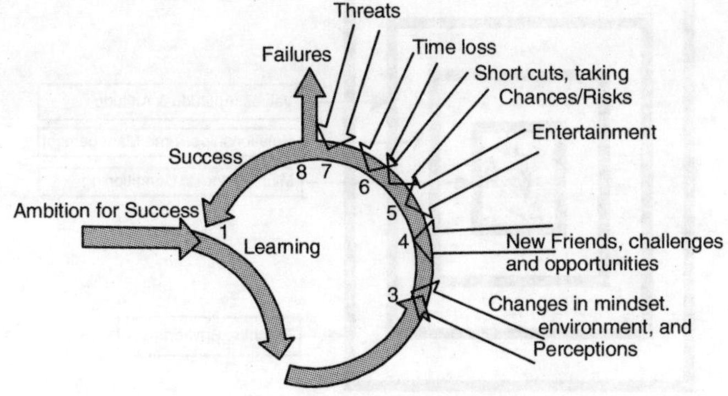

Hurdles in Realising Success

the learning. The whole experience could be a fun or tough (or both) depending upon the attitude, personal management, experience and the external environment. One may face the threat of loosing the direction, the purpose and getting disorganized and fragmented in thoughts and actions.

This leads us to the idea—"organize your thinking". Make this the idea of your life. Live on the idea. Let every thought be organized. This will convert your dream into plans and actions, where time, space, relationships and management become the resources. This is a way to success. This is power learning, lifelong learning. Some call it factor four techniques where you invest half of the time/resources and learn twice. The process comprises the following 8 steps:

1. Cleaning, de-cluttering, emptying, opening locks, unlearning
2. See, observe, retain childlike curiosity, focus
3. Listen, sharpen the knive, meditate
4. Understand, digest, penetrate, assimilate, categorise, synthesise
5. Rigour, be exact and delivery oriented
6. Values
7. Active learning and professional attitude
8. Lifelong learning, refine, review, experiment

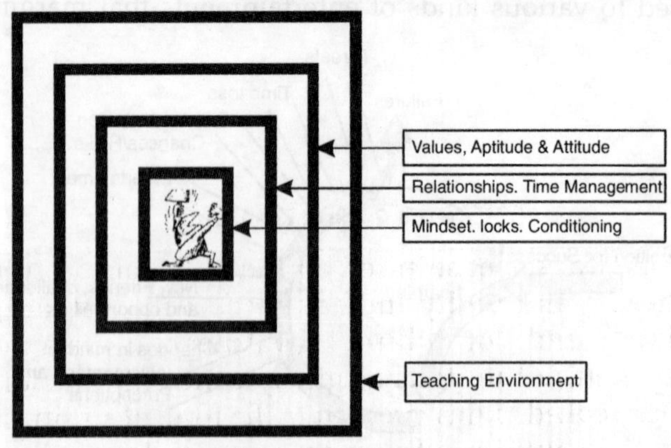

Barriers to Learning

Inequities in Access to Learning

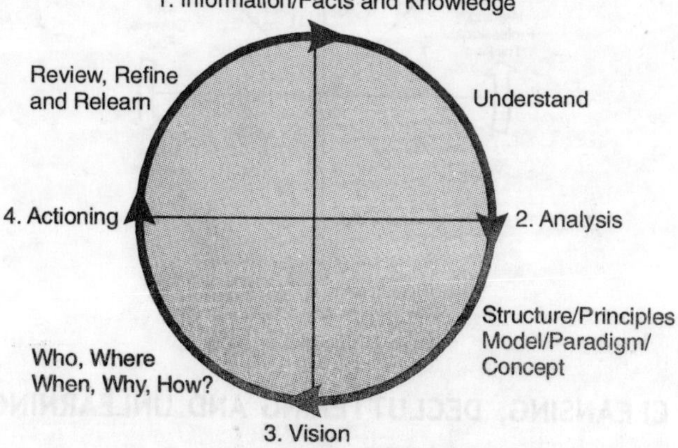

Barm's Cycle of Learning

In America, someone asked an Indian scholar in a big gathering as to why Indians were poor, lethargic, backward and slow whereas the Americans were rich, prosperous, fast and technologically advanced. The Indian scholar replied to this question in the form of a story. He said, There were two fishemen, one was American and the other Indian. One day they were fishing at the same sea-shore by chance. The American fisherman asked his Indian counterpait, "My brother, why are you fishing by this primitive method, catching fish by a string. Why don't you use machine like me?" The Indian fisherman then asked, "Then what would happen?" The American exclaimed, "Then what would happen? You would catch the fish in one catch, you take the whole day". The Indian again asked, Then what would happen?" The American replied, "Then you would amass lot of money, riches, properties, investments, etc." Again the Indian asked, "Then what would happen?" The American replied, "Then you would relax." The Indian said "That is what I am doing now".

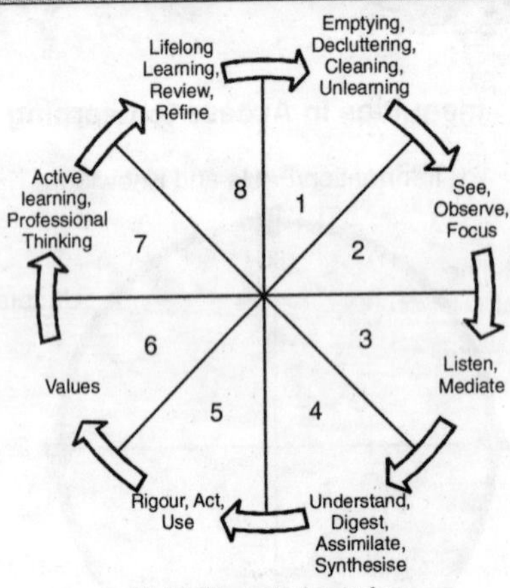

Eight Steps to Learning

CLEANSING, DECLUTTERING AND UNLEARNING

जाड्यं धियो हरतसिञ्चितिवायसित्यं
मानोन्नतदिशितिपापमाकरोति।
चेतः प्रसादयतदिकिषु तनोतिकीर्तिं।
सत्संगतिः कथय कनि करोतपुंसाम्॥

"Knowledge removes lethargy of the intellect, invests truth in the speech, enhances the greatness and casts off sin; cleanse the mind and spreads the fame all around." **Bhirthrihari**

Most of us have certain attitudes, which lock our thinking into the *status quo* and close the mind. They get in the way of learning and being creative. These are mental blocks. Today, information technology (IT) has opened up the floodgates of fast knowledge and diversions. The explosion of communication, entertainment, connections and the noise keep the students distracting. For a serious student, there is need to de-clutter the mind, cleanse it and give it the rest by restricted use of mobile, internet, TV, etc. Eliminate and forget what is not necessary, disturbing or overtaking you. Hobbies, physical activities, deep breathing, meditation and positive thoughts help in de-cluttering and opening up of mental locks and blocks.

We Wash and Purify our Body Everyday, but Often Forget to Cleanse Our Mind

Two monks who had renounced the world and taken vows of celibacy and simplicity. One monk was older and the other was relatively young. They were wandering in the forest one day and came upon a rushing river. On the edge of the river stood a beautiful young woman. Her face as marked by anxiety as she explained to the monks that she needed to get across but it was rushing too fast and she was afraid. She humbly requested the monks if one of them would be good enough to carry her across. The older monk immediately picked her up gallantly and carried her to the other side while the younger monk walked by his side. Upon reaching the other shore, the monk placed the woman safely on the ground, and they bid her farewell.

One week later the two monks were sitting under a tree for their morning meditations when the younger monk suddenly exclaimed, "Okay, I've been keeping this inside for the last week but I cannot keep it inside anymore. I cannot believe the way you picked up that young, beautiful woman and carried her body so close to yours. After taking vows of celibacy before God, after promising to forsake the touch of a woman, how could you wrap your arms around her body and carry her tightly in your arms? I have had such respect, even reverence for you for so many years, and now I feel so betrayed. You are not a true monk! You are not a true celibate. I must find another companion with whom I can tread a path of purity."

The elder monk listened with a faint smile growing across his face. "My brother," he said when the younger monk had finished his tirade. "I carried that young woman in my arm for approximately 2 minutes and left her by the side of the river, after setting her down safely. She has not been with me since. You, on the other hand, have carried her in your heart for the last week, you have slept with her, eaten with her, breathed with her and even meditated with her because you cannot get her out of your mind. She is living permanently in your heart. It is your own heart you must seek to purify, not the actions of your travelling companions."

On unlearning, Nobel Prize Winner Leo Esaki (who won the prize for his work with transistor tunnel effects) offered *Five Things Not To Do To Be a Nobel Prize Winner.*

Five Things Not to Do to Be a Nobel Prize Winner

1. Do not allow yourself to be trapped by your past experiences.
2. Do not allow yourself to be overly attached to any authority.
3. Do not hold onto what you don't need.
4. Do not avoid confrontation.
5. Do not lose chidhood curioslty in everyday life.

It is rare that childlike curiosity is retained in later life. This gives ability to think original. This to clear from these examples from the history of painting:

- Michelangelo used the perspective approach. If one looks at the painting of "The Last Supper," one can see it was done using perspective lines. The painter is using objective measurement to draw beauty from an outside perspective.
- The impressionists, like Monet during the industrial revolution jumped in and swam in nature. They left the studio and went outside into nature. Their

paintings show the steam of locomotives in the background of the scene, iron fences, and bridges, steam and iron being symbols of modernity in the time of the impressionists.

- The abstractionists, like Picasso, went further. They swam in nature, jumped out, and painted what they saw. The purpose of their paintings was not to copy nature but rather to show the viewer the sentiment, emotion, and concept the artist saw in nature.

One has to be ready to learn. A pitcher should be empty to be filled up:

Once a youngman approached Ramakrishna Paramahamsa, wanting to be his disciple. But the sage answered cryptically, "Knowledge isn't important, readiness is." The youngman promptly replied, "I am ready." To which the sage replied, "Let me be the judge." A day, then two and then a week passed. But the youngman was no closer to being initiated. Then, one day, Ramakrishna told him to accompany him as he went to the river for a bath. Thrilled, the youngman eagerly followed.

When Ramakrishna reached the river, he suddenly held the lad by the scruff of his neck and pushed his head under water. The boy thrashed, struggled, screamed and yelled, until finally he broke free. He then spluttered, "Why did you do that I couldn't breathe. I was gasping for air." "Now, were you?" Ramakrishna asked, as if surprised. Quietly, he added, "But that's because you can't live without air. One day, when you gasp for knowledge as desperately as you now gasped for air, why, only then, will you be ready for knowledge."

The libraries are like the mountains—full of precious minerals, metals and gems. However, every indivdual has to discover, pick up and polish them according to his own need and taste. One has to empty the container in order to fill it up.

A sage always pointed to a book he carried with him, saying that all he was doing was quoting from that book. Try as they would they could never get the sage to part with the book or even reveal its name to them. Then, one day, the sage died. Before doing so, he handed over the book to his disciple saying, "Open it when I have passed on."

Eagerly, the students picked up the book on the death of the master. The book contained only one page and that page only one sentence, "When you understand the difference between the container and the content, the fount of wisdom will open to you."

Meditation Improves Brain Wiring

What the saints and *yoga gurus* had been saying since ages, had been verified by a new study that meditation can alter your brain wiring within a month that could lead to the treatment of mental disorders. Scientists in the US looked at the effect of integrative body-mind training (IBMT) of two groups of university students and found significant physical changes in their brains after just four weeks in 11 hours of training. *Pranayam* also helps in cleansing the mind, *brithhari* exercise is simple and quick. Inhale air quickly and exhale with a force through the nose about 10 times everyday. This exercise will cleanse the brain of toxins.

Patanjali's *yoga* is called *Ashtanga Yoga* which literally means 'eight-limbed *yoga*'. The heart of his teachings are incorporated in the 'eight-fold path'. According to Patanjali, the path of internal purification for revealing the Universal Self consists of eight practices:

1. **Yama:** attitude towards our environment, discipline, self-control
2. **Niyama:** attitude towards ourselves
3. **Asana:** the practice of body exercise
4. **Pranayama:** the practice of breathing exercise
5. **Prathyahara:** the restraint of our senses
6. **Dharana:** the ability to direct the mind
7. **Dhyana:** the ability to develop interaction with what we seek to understand
8. **Samadhi:** complete itegration with the object to be understood.

I think, therefore I am. —*Descartes*

Seeing:

In the following passage from the *Chhandogya Upanishad*, Shvetaketu is seeking answers.

'Please Sir, tell me more of this teaching,' said the boy.

'Very well, my son. Go and pick a fig from the banyan tree.'

'Here you are, sir.'

'Split it open and tell me what you see inside.'

'Many tiny seeds, sir.'

'Take one of them and split it open and tell me what you see inside.'

'Nothing at all, sir.'

Then the father said, 'The subtlest essence of the fig. appears to you as nothing, but, believe me my son, from that very nothing this mighty banyan tree has arisen.

That being which is the subtlest essence of everything, the supreme reality, the Self of all that exists. That art Thou, *Shvetaketu*.'

There are many 'Ways of Seeing', but in our own tradition, *drishti*, with all its varied meanings and subtle shades, has also many levels, and it is with these that *sanskriti*, culture, engages itself all at once: seeing, beholding, using the mind's eye and intelligence, having an insight into things, views, systems. Then when all this is done not in a dry, academic way, but using, in Coomaraswamy's seductive phrase, 'the transfiguring eyes of love', things begin to change, and hearts to move.

Drishti, f. seeing, viewing, beholding (also with the mental eye); . . . sight, the faculty of seeing; . . .the mind's eye, wisdom, intelligence; . . . view,theory, doctrine, system, . . . aspect of the stars...

Drishtin, mfn. having an insight into or familiar with anything; having the looks or thoughts directed upon anything.

–Monier Williams, *A Sanskrit - English Dictionary*

Perceptions are as important as reality - people may be wrong about you, a problem, or your work effort but you have to deal with their perceptions. Vision is seeing something which is not visible.

Arjuna was the only one, amongst all the student archers, who, when asked to shoot a bird said, "I see nothing but the eye of the bird," every other pupil had seen everything from the jungle to the trees to the branches. Guru Drona was able to deduce the ability to see in the lad that would one day make him the best archer in the world. He saw that Arjuna, alone of all the students, could see and focus.

In the journey of knowledge (*gyan*) the first step is to be awake and open the eyes. By 'seeing, one becomes a 'seer'. Einstein could see energy in matter and Newton could see gravitational force in a falling apple. Get up, awake and open the eyes to embark upon the journey.

> *If one is trying to do something really well one becomes, first of all interested in it, and later absorbed in it, which means that one forgets oneself in concentrating on what one is doing. But when one forgets oneself, oneself ceases to exist, since oneself is the only thing which causes oneself to exist.*
>
> **—Christmas Humphreys, *Concentration and Meditation***

A group of people decided to go and look at the beauty of the sunest. The scientist saw only the formation of clouds, the astronomer the position of the stars, the environmentalist, the pollution of the atmosphere, the fashion designer, the colours of the sky. The child when asked what he saw said, "I saw the Sun smile". The problem was not in the object, the problem was in the seeing. For you can only see what your perception allows you to see.

A philosopher who, after having studied extensively, decided to visit his village. Stuffed with pedantic thought and with an exaggerated sense of his own importance, he stood at the riverbank, waiting to cross the river to his village. Soon, he was seated in the boat that would take him across. He looked scornfully at the boatman. Toiling hard to row the boat, and asked, "Do you know anything of philosophy?" "No" "Then a quarter of your life has been lost," He said with a sad shake of his head, "Have you been to school?" "No." "Then half of your life has been lost, "exclaimed the scholar. A while later, he asked, "Do you at least know to read or write?" "No". "Ah! Dear man, three-fourths of your life is lost." Suddenly the boat began to rock. The water started rising. It seemed that a storm was brewing. The boatman, prepared to jump into the river and asked, "Do you know how to swim?" "Not at all!" said the scholar. "Sir, I am sorry to say, your entire life will soon be lost." With that the boatman swam his way shoreward.

Right knowledge is all pervading and omnipresent, which needs cultivating the right vision. Lack of right perception makes the learning difficult, as it creates false fears and illusions. This is clear in the following story:

A king was looking for a suitable candidate for the post of prime minister. After several tests, three people were shortlisted. The next day was the final test. There was a rumour that the king had a magic lock which can be opened only with great skill and knowledge. And whoever unlocked it, would be the prime minister.

Hearing the rumour, two of the selected candidates acquired a lot of books on locks. They spent the whole night going through the mathematical equations relalting to locks. The third person was very relaxed. The next morning, all three were taken to the palace. And the rumour turned out to be true. The king said whoever unlocks the lock will be prime minister.

These two people felt very happy thinking that it was good that they had referred to many books and then went and looked at the lock. Once again they returned to the books, whereas the third person, looking relaxed, went there, looked at the lock and pulled it, and to his surprise, it opened. In fact, it was not locked at all. The other two were still busy referring to books.

In the meantime, the king announced that the third person had been selected as prime minister. The other two asked him, "You never referred to any book on locks, how did you unlock it?" The king said, "The very first thing that a prime minister should do is that he should know whether the problem really exists or not, before trying to solve it."

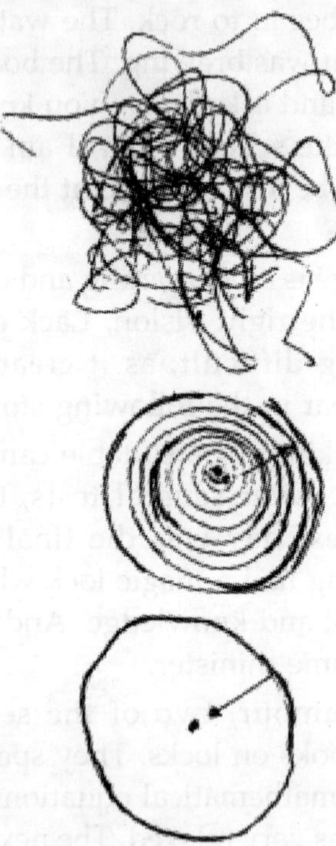

A point in space as an organizing idea. Paul Klee sketch (*The Thinking Eye*). The artist has very clearly explained the process of focusing and organising throughts from a chaotic state of mind.

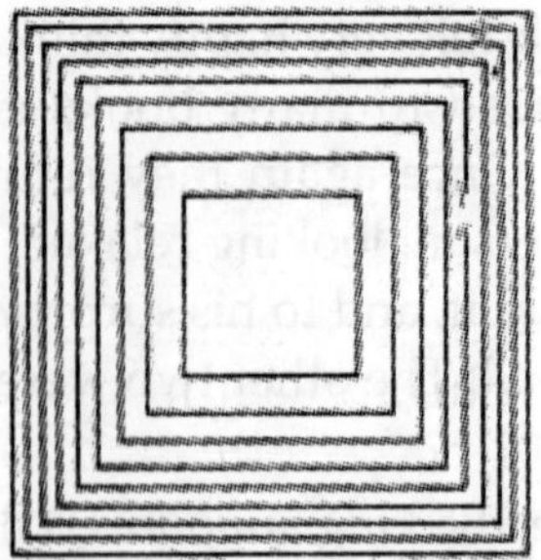

Fresnel's diagram. The outer band has exactly the same area as the central square, an important principle in relation to the way in which buildings are placed on the land.

Site covered with pavilions (left) or courts (right). The area covered by black and whites is equal.

Focus

Concentrate attention on process and targets, as sports psychologist Jerry May, while working for the U.S. Olympic Sailing Team, explained:

> I don't think people achieve just by serendipity. If you have visions of what you would like to focus on and accomplish, you have to come up with ways of getting there. I don't want to overstructure goals, but in sailing, if you want to be a great sailor, you need to be thinking about what you want to achieve. We call those "wish goals". The media, the public, and athletes tend to measure sports by those goals. They're okay, but they're overemphasized. Examples are: "I want to win a gold medal" or "I want to be in the top five in this next regatta." Although they may help motivate you, just sitting around wishing about those goals does nothing to achieve them. "Task goals" are the ones that need more attention. These are skill development goals. The sailing coaches and I met, and we came up with six areas where they they'd like to see athletes focus on taks goals: Sailing technique (such as boat speed and boat handling), racing technique (starting and tactics), physical conditioning, mental skills (such as understanding your arousal level and proper focus), organization (like boat and equipment selection), and personal goals. The last one is a concept I discuss with anyone who is in top level competition and a high-achiever, whether they are business people, medical students, or athletes. We must find time for personal relationships,

education and other kinds of career goals and recreation.

Without focus and plans to reach the goal, you are like a ship that has set sail with no destination. Often a learner gets entangled, with the tools and vehicle he/she would forget the goal. The student becomes seeker and a seer when he keeps in focus the goal.

An ardent devotee decided that he would get down to the secret behind his guru's great wisdom. So, he kept a watch over the guru's every action. He saw that before every session with his disciples, the master would take out a book. Then, he would go to his personal shrine, and removing a pen from it, write something into the book, soon after, with deep reverence and respect, he would place the pen back in a silken pouch from where he had taken it. The disciple was convinved that *that* was where the wisdom lay.

So, one day, in great stealth, he stole the pen from its place of worship, ran up to his room and with great excitement, drew to a paper to write. He was sure, pearls of wisodm would drop and he would be proclaimed as the next master. After all, wasn't the pen the secret of his guru's greatness? He sat for an hour, and then two. Nothing happened. Suddenly, behind him, he heard a whisper, "Son, it isn't in the pen. It is inside. The pen, the flute, the bulb are merely conduits. The light is always within - in the realm of the soul, the living consciousness."

Learning the obvious is easy. It can be taught. Beyond information and knowledge, one has to learn by himself. This is discovered in silence, in meditation and is beyond words.

Multiview

We need explicit methods to become more open observers and discover the multiview. The following rules-of-thumb need to be understood:

(*i*) First, defer assessments about the viewpoints of others; try to understand the other person's point of view.

(*ii*) Second, it helps to note down what the other person says, digest it before reacting.

(*iii*) To find the multiview, we have to become more *open*, understand how others see things, and why their perspective on the situation makes sense.

People have a strong tendency to use two-valued or 0-1 thinking ("It's a hot day," "the city is polluted"). The two-valued scale is very gross, and it is unclear what the boundary between the two values means.

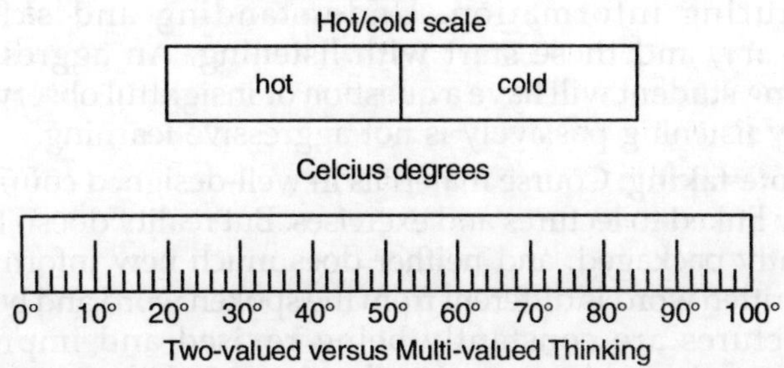

Two-valued versus Multi-valued Thinking

Two-valued thinking is often a rehetoric or demagoguery. It simplifies the situation to the point of non-reality, and people delude themselves ("our education is the best and doesn't need improvement").

Multi-valued thought and speech is the tool of those trying to understand a real situation and initiate effective corrective action. Multi-valued thought uses a scale with fine gradations and precise location of the values.

Different observers see the same situation differently. How a person sees a situation says more about the person's way of observing and about the person than about the situation. This is a key idea. If we are to understand the various concerns of people, we must break out of the mindset that how we see something is how it is and that the other person's viewpoint or concern is wrong. We must try to validate the perspectives of others - to understand how they see the situation so we can understand them.

What we can physiologically observe is our emotional state; our experiences; the vocabulary we have and how we understand language; individual beliefs and mental models; automatic ways of reacting to things; and cultural background. Each of us makes assumptions that are so natural to us that, not ony do we often fail to explain our assumptions to someone else, we are often not even conscious of them ourselves.

Some of the way we observe things is visible to others like the tip of an ice-berg. However, much of the way we observe things is invisible to others and often partly invisible to ourselves as well. What we don't see, we still get. The observer-that-one-is is inside us all the time influencing how we reason.

Listening and Learning

One skill often neglected in the learning is capturing and structuring information. Understanding and skill are necessary, and these start with listening. An aggressively listening student will have a question or insightful observation. Simply listening passively is not aggressive learning.

Note-taking: Course materials in well-designed courses are closely linked to lectures and exercises. But reality doesn't come so neatly packaged, and neither does much new information. The written word is different from the spoken word and because the lectures are constantly being revised and improved. Therefore, the students need to develop the skill of *note-taking*. This will sharpen their focus ont the information, preserve knowledge and demonstrate interest and concern for the presenters. In addition, by disciplining themselves to take effective notes, the students acquire a useful skill.

Awakening: Swami Chinmayananda gives the following perception of awakening:

> "To forget oneself totally, one's mind should keep awake at every moment. A mind that has forgotten the past and the future, that is awake to the now, to the present, expresses the highest concentration of intelligence. It is alert, it is watchful, it is inspired. The actions of a person who has such a mind are exceptionally creative and perfect. Verliy to forget onseself totally, is to be in perfection."

Awakening menifests belief in self and discovery of one's own potentials

Wings to Fly

You were born with potential.
You were born with goodness and trust.
You were born with ideas and dreams.
You were born with greatness.
You were born with wings.
You are not meant for crawling,
So I don't,
I have wings.
I will Learn to use them to fly.

—Jalaluddin Rumi
13th Century Persian Sufi Poet

The message is that education gives you wings to fly. Achievement comes from self-belief that "I will win." What is needed is the culture of excellence and performance.

Be Silent and Listen

samyaya uvaca
evam uktva hṛsikesam
gudakesah paramtapah
na yotstya iti govndam
uktva tusnim babhuva ha

Samjaya said:

Having thus addressed Hrisikesa (Krishna), the mighty Gudakesa (Arjuna) said to Govinda (Krishna) "I will not fight" and became silent.

Na yotsye: "I will not fight." Arjuna, without waiting for the advice of the teacher, seems to have made up his mind. While he asks the teacher to advise him, his mind is not open. The task of the teacher becomes more difficult.

Govinda: The omniscience of the teacher is indicated by this word, *Madhusudana.*

Tusnim babhuva: become silent. The voice of truth can be heard only in silence.

Bhagavad Gita
Chapter 2: 8-9

Today, in a talkative world one has forgotten the importance of silence. It is in 'silent' state one can learn and realise the truth. In fact the term 'muni' comes from 'mouni, that is, one who has taken vow not to speak. The famous conversation in silence between Kabir and Farid is explicit:

> Once Farid came to India to meet Kabir and they lived together for three days. Both of them did not ever speak to each other, yet they were happy to be together. When Farid left Kabir, his disciples asked him as to why they did not talk as it was a very good opportunity for both the mystics to exchange ideas. Kabir said that they had talked enough, but in silence.

Enlarging Understanding

One learns according to his own measure and perceptions. A narrow extent of the understanding and knowledge is the reason of the suffering, disputes and tensions. The purpose of knowledge is 'expansion' of the container, the mind and the world. The Zen Master narrates the virute of expansion in this story beautifully:

> A Zen Master has a disciple who was perpetually unhappy and dissatisfied. One day the disciple approached the Master and said "Master bless me too with your wisdom and help me find happiness." The old master instructed the unhappy young man to put handful of salt in glass of warm water and drink it. "How does it taste?" The Master asked. "Awful", spat the young man. The Master chuckled and then asked the young man to take another handful of salt and put it in the lake. Two walked in silence to the nearby lake and when the young man swirled his handful of salt into the lake, the Master said, "now drink from the lake." As the water dripped down the young man's chin, the Master asked, "How does it taste." "Good" remarked the young man. "Do you taste the salt?" asked the Master. "No", said the young man. The Master sat besides this troubled young man, took his hand and said, "Pain of life is pure salt; no more, no less. The amount of pain in life remains the same, exactly the same. But amount we taste the 'pain' depends on the container we put it into. So when you are in pain, the only thing you can do is to enlarge your sense of things. Stop being a glass. Become a lake."

One has to make effort to understand and appreciate while it needs no understanding to criticise:

> Once there were three men sitting under a tree in the garden and they started talking about God. One man said, I don't believe that God is perfect. In fact, three are so many things which even an ordinary reasonable man would be able to plan better than God. For example look over there. The man drew his friends' attention to the pumpkin patch where hundreds of pumpkins were growing large and round. "God has put these huge, heavy

pumpkins on the end of tiny, thin vines which always collapse under the weight of their enormous fruit."

One of the other men joined in, "Yes, you're right," he said. "Look there at the mango trees. Huge, strong, sturdy trees. And their fruit? A tiny 4 ounce mango! What kind of backward planning is this? Put the heavy fruit on the thin weak vine and put the light fruit on the tall strong tree? I agree that God definitely is far from perfect."

However, the third man was unpersuaded. "What you both are saying certainly is compelling. You are right that it might have made more sense to put the heavy fruit on the strong tree and the light fruit on the thin vine, but still I believe that there must be a bigger, better, divine plan. I still believe that God knows exactly what He's doing and that His planning is perfect even if we don't understand it."

The two friends chided the third for his simplicity and blind faith. "Can't you see with your own eyes how stupid it is? Even an idiot would know better!"

Wounded by the other men's criticism, yet secure in his faith, the third man stood up and went to rest under a nearby three, separate from his two critical friends. All three drifted off into a deep afternoon slumber in the shade of the mango trees.

With the afternoon clouds, a strong wind rose up and whipped through the trees. Branches swayed in the heavy wind, causing ripe mangoes to fall to the ground. The sleeping skeptics awoke, startled by mangoes falling on them.

One of them exclaimed, "Our friend the believer was right! It is certainly a good thing that only mangoes hang from these branches. The weight of a falling mango was enough to startle me from sleep and bruise my cheek. Had it been heavy pumpkins falling onto us we would have become pumpkin pie! It is very good those heavy pumpkins grow so close to the ground!"

5 Ws and 1 H for Understanding: The learning method includes the concept of the *5 Ws and 1 H* - who, what, where, when, why, and how. One uses four of these Ws (who, what, where, when) and the one H to dig for detail, emotion and dissect inference and judgment to get to the underlying facts and guide statements down the ladder of abstraction.

Who : Who does it, who should do it, who else can do it?

What : What to do, what is being done, what can be done?

Where : Where to do it, where is it done, where else should it be done?

When : When to do it, when is it done, when else should it be done?

How : How to do it, how is it done, how should it be done, how can this method be used elsewhere?

> *"Don't keep forever on the public road, going only where others have gone. Leave the beaten track occasionally and dive into the woods. You will be certain to find something you have never seen before. It will be a little thing, but do not ignore it. Follow it up, explore all around it; one discovery will leald to another, and before you know it, you will have something worth thinking about."*
>
> **—Alexander Graham Bell (1905)**

Rigour, Dogged Persistence

All of the great scientists engaged in repeated, detailed investigations and experiments had many failures before they had their breakthroughs. Edison purportedly said: "if you want more successes, you have to have more failures." Pasteur said, "in the natural sciences, success only favours the well prepared," and more than one person has said: "the harder I work, the luckier I get." Big breaks from past business practices may be required; people may have flashed of inspiration. However, persistence and organization will undoubtedly be required. Continuous improvement is a means of break through. In fact, a most impressive characteristic of a scientist is dogged persistence, through routine and setbacks, until he finally succeeds.

The sages have taught that:

> "If one is trying to do something really well one becomes, first of all interested in it, and later absorbed in it, which means that one forgets oneself in concentrating on what one is doing. But when one forgets oneself, oneself ceases to exist, since oneself is the only thing which causes oneself to exist."

> *It is one of the strange ironies of this strange life that those who work the hardest, who subject themselves to the strictest discipline, who give up certain pleasurable things in order to achieve a goal, are the happiest people.*
>
> **—Brutus Hamilton**

Recently, I heard the remark of a respected senior engineer that in his time there was no money but lot of professional respect and now it is *vice versa*. There is no doubt about the truth or this statement. However, it is also true that Lakshmi and Saraswati have never been great friend. The Brahmins, the intelligentia of the traditional society, have always been paupers or bhikshus.

It is famously said that:

"if you think you're tops, you won't do much climbing."
Brilliance is 90 per cent perspiraton.

> *"My family is not poor, but we have been brought up to be frugal. My parents and I live in the same house that my paternal grandparents moved into after World War II in 1945. It is a big house by today's standards,but it is simple.Those who see it for the first time are astonished that Minister Mentor Lee Kuan Yew's home is so humble. But it is a comfortable house . . . Though it does look shabby compared to the new mansions on our street, we are not bothered by the comparison . . . Being wealthy is not a sin. It cannot be in a capitalist market economy. Enjoying the fruits of one's own labour is one's prerogative and I have no right to chastise those who choose to live luxuriously.*

> *But neither an Aston Martin nor an Hermes Birkin can make us truly contented . . . When the end approaches and we look back . . . will we regret the latest phone or car that we did not acquire? Or would we prefer to die at peace with ourselves, knowing that our lives were filled with love, friendship and goodwill?"*
>
> **—Lee W Ling,**
> **National Neuroscience Institute, Singapore**

Values

> Your work is to discover your world and then with all your heart give yourself to it.
>
> **—Gautama Buddha**

Mahatma Gandhi said: "The real difficulty is that people have no idea of what education truly is. We assess the value of education in the same manner as we assess the value of land or of shares in the stock-exchange market. We want to provide only such education as would enable the student to earn more. We hardly give any thought to the improvement of the character of the educated. The girls, we say, do not have to earn: so why should they be educated? As long as such ideas persist there is no hope of our ever knowing the true value of education". In the connected world where we live, it is imperative that education is treated as the only glue that can ensure that the world flourished. Education iteself is a best practice that can happen in ones life. It should teach us humility and benevolence and a clarity of mind and purpose. Mathematicians have sought knowledge in figures, Philospophers in systems, Logicians in subtleties, and Metaphysicians in sounds. It is not in any, nor in all of these. One who studies only men will get the body of knowledge without the soul, and he that studies only books, the soul without the body. In the ultimate analysis an educational system isn't worth a great deal if it teaches young to make a living but doesn't teach them how to make a life. As Anne Sullivan who hereself was blind, and taught Helen Keller as a child, said "I am beginning to suspect all elaborate and special systems of education. They seem to me to be built up on the supposition that every child is a king of idiot who must be taught to think." We need a paradigm that changes education to knowledge of the world around us. It should develop in a perspective of looking at life and help us build opnions and points of view on life. Information can be converted into knowledge with education as a catalyst.

The father of a young man went on a tour for a few days explaining to his son that he should take care of the garden, he had beautifully maintained and should properly water the plants and flowers. When the father returned back from his tour, he noticed to his shock that all those beautiful plants and flowers have almost died. He rebuked his son and asked why he did not obey his instructions. The boy replied, "I did father, I daily used to sprinkle water over plant, branch and flower and sometimes I even sprinkled the fragrance which I brought from Paris. What can I do, even then are dying?" The father then asked, "Did you put the water in the roots of the plants?" The son said. "No. That I did not do, but I am telling you the truth that daily I used to put the water over the plants, branches and all the flowers, but it did not occur to me that I have to put water in the roots." The father exclaimed, "All that was useless. You should have looked to the roots. Never forget the roots."

> *"All things are connected. This we know. The earth does not belong to man; man belongs to the Earth. All things are connected, like the blood which unites one family. Whatever befalls the earth befalls the sons and daughters of the earth. Man did not weave the web of life, he is merely a strand in it. Whatever he does to the web, he does to himself."*
>
> **Native American, Chief, Seattle, (nearly 200 years ago)**

Active Learning

The only thing that interferes with my learning is my education.

—Albert Einstein

Learning is an active process and process of change - in attitudes, understanding, skills and behaviour. Studies indicate that learning is most likely to occur when people have participated actively in the process. Participatory active learning has various forms such as group discussion, seminars, quiz, roundtable, etc. It aims at:

- Stimulating interest, personal involvement and relationships
- Clarifying the thinking of the individual by real life experiences and examples
- Providing the means of testing and evaluating one's ideas
- Helping one to see different ways of looking at one's ideas and arguments
- Providing instant feedback
- Pooling knowledge.

Some of the useful tools of participatory learning are:

- Team building,
- Humour,
- Graphics,
- Matrix charts,
- Case studies,
- Quiz,
- Metaphors,
- Anecodotes,
- Objective-subjective interface, and,
- Story-line.

Learning and problem solving process invloves:

- The statement of the problem
- The analysis of the problem
- The collection of relevant facts
- The development of alternative solutions
- The testing of facts against proposed solutions
- The assessment of available resources
- The plan of action - who will do what, when, where, and how.

Without goals and plans to reach there, you are like a ship that has set a sail with no destination.

—Fitzhugh Dodson

Learning cannot be imposed on students but must be a common journey led by the students themselves. In an experiment, attempting to change the cooking and food habits of the housewives in World War II, one group of women was given lecture on the advantages of new food and the way of preparing them. Another group participated in a group discussion on the same subject. The result was that only 3% of the first group changed their food habits while 30% of those who had participated in the group discussion changed their food habit.

Learning involves investment of time, energy, finances and other resources. The same student learns many times by active participatory method than in a routine lecture examination style. This implies that method of learning and teachng is crucial. It makes all the difference. This is why IIMs, Harvard, INSEAD and some other institutes have become the brand names while many other institutes are struggling to emulate their success story. Any amount of advertisement and publicity is not going to make much difference. What needs to done is to adopt new ways of teaching and learning, where student picks up the maximum in the available time. The fear of attendance should not make a student to sit in the class, but s/he is motivated and gets interested in the subject and develop an urge, a thirst to learn.

Soft and Hard Mediums

According to the Roger Van Dech (A Whack on a side of the head) things are not always black or white, but there are many shades of grey, or different colours. A few might say that you can pick up the things on the hard side-like bar of metal, the soft things are little more difficult to grab-lke water. Soft thinking has many of the characteristics on the soft list. It is metaphorical, approximate, diffuse, humourous, playful and capable of dealing with contradictions. Hard thinking on the

Source: www.digitallearning.in

Knowledge is what drives today's world. Centres of higher learning like professional colleges, engineering institutes and management schools are constantly looking at new ways to stay competitive and relevant in the changing learning landscape. Information Technology is a key driver and differentiator in today's world. Research shows that students who have regular access to interactive learning methods retain and grasp better and have an edge over their peers.

other hand, tends to be more logical, precise, exact, specific and consistent. It is like a spotlight-bright, clear and intense, however, the focus is narrow. Soft thinking is like a floodlight. It is more diffuse, not as intense, but covers a wider area. Soft teaching methods educate the student by triggering his own thinking and search for connections among things, rather than on their differences. Every Indian has the backgroud (*sanskar*) of soft thinking - mythology, metaphors, dreams, poetry, play, etc., which can be usefully employed in teaching, cross-breeded with hard mediums. The objective of learning is to convert a layman's mind into professional way of thinking.

Soft and Hard Mediums of Learning

Soft	Hard
Metaphor	Logic
Dream	Reason
Humour	Precision
Ambiguity	Consistency
Play	Work
Approximate	Exact
Fantasy	Reality
Paradox	Direct
Diffuse	Focused
Hunch	Analysis
Generalization	Specifics

"As we know there are known knowns. There are things we know. We also know that there are known unknowns. That is to say that we know that there are something we do not know. But there are also unknown unknowns. The one's we don't know that we don't know."

Donald Rumfield, US Secretary of Defence

Difference Between a Professional and Non-professional/Layman

Professional	Non-Professional Layman
Position as it is	Judgemental, temperamental
Open, fresh and clear mind	Personal preferences/likings
Observation	Prejudices
Simplifying the complex	Complicating simple things
Originality	Relies on popular media, hackneyed knowledge
Understanding, process, learning	Borrowed teaching, correcting
Facts and figure	Weak facts, figures and fictions
Empirical analysis, logic	Default logic, fault finding
Conceptualisation	Winding statements, piecemeal ideas
Forming right questions	Jumping to conclusions and anwers
Relate to context, specifics	Generalisation
See positive side, learn from success	Over critical, learn from failures
Continuity, clairity of communication	Ad-hoc statements, jumps and jerks
Aggregation, big picture	Fragmentation, picemeal, disjointed

Professional	Non-Professional Layman
Objective	Subjective, image worship
Literature scanning, references, credits	Poor reading, no references, no credit
Structured thinking	Flesh without bones, cosmetic
Honest, practical, examples, illustrations	Too verbose, literary/jargons
Evolving, innovative, transformative	Rigid, fixed

Let us end this chapter with a little humour.

Three gentlemen arrived together at the Pearly Gates and were informed there was only room for one. They decided that the man with the oldest profession would be the one allwoed to come in. The first stepped froward and said, "The Lord made Adam and then created Eve out of a rib from Adam and that took surgery. I am a surgeon, so I guess it's me". But before he could move in, the second one said, "Wait, Before the Lord did that, he worked six days. Everything was Chaos and he worked six days and created Earth. That makes him an engineer. I'm an engineer, so I guess that calls for me." Then the third one stepped up and said, "Hold on a minute. I'm a manger who do you think made all that chaos?"

CHAPTER 3

Participatory Learning

भवन्तनिम्रास्तरवः फलोद्गमैः
नवाम्बुभर्मिरुविलिम्बिनो घनाः।
अनुद्धताः सतपुरुषाः समृद्धिभिः
स्वभाव एवैषः परोपकारणिाम्॥

With fruits, trees bend, that is be humble, with water clouds hang long, that is wealthy good men maintain humble posture and are seen to be benevolent.

—*Bhrithrihari in Shatakatrayi*

Brithrihavi epic makes a clear distribution between learning and teaching:

"Learning is the greater personality of man; it is his hidden and safely deposited wealth; it is the teacher of teachers; it is a kinsman. Learning promotes an indescribable happiness at all times."

The traditional classroom learning environment, in which an instructor talks and students listen and then do homewerk, differs greatly from work environment. In classrooms students learn primarily from the instructor and from the teaching materials provided. But the most common learning is in the groups in which no one is much more knowledgeable than the others. The purpose of participatory or group learning is to get in students involved and realize the synergy of group thinking, action and behaviour. This way they tend to become more self-reliant, articulate and self-starting.

One school of academic thought encourages teaching to give minimal guidance to the students, so the students can develop the skill of discovering things on their own. The students are expected to experiment with variations and try out self-learning. This approach can speed up the conversion of knowledge into understanding. At the stage where understanding is turned into skills, however, it is less useful. Encouraging individual variations in the beginning of the learning may slow down progress considerably and needs careful guidance and facilitation by a structured programme.

As stated by Benjamin Franklin, the purpose of participatory learning is to involve the student "Tell me and I forget. Teach me and I remember. Involve me and I learn."

Participatory learning is a means of team building, stimulating lateral thinking. The students are more likely to learn if they are involved in democratic group discussion. It may sometimes seem easier to teach by traditional lectures and ensure attendance by coercion. In the long run, however, learning and group thinking are more efficient, because the students learn by doing, even from their mistakes, and sovle the problems. However, group learning is not:

- a debate;
- a speech;
- an argument;
- a conversation;
- an opinion poll;
- an opportunity to air prejudices.

Participatory learning requires following certain rules of the game, arrangements and an organizational structure, where every student is encouraged to participate, think, learn and speak-up. It is worthwhile to mention six things which each student should do:

- **Speak up** - when you have something to contribute but not just to hear your own voice
- **Do not interrupt** - when someone else is speaking. If your idea is worthwhile its value will not depreciate in two or three minutes.
- **Listen carefully** - especially if you do not agree with everything which is being said.
- **Be brief/concise and objective** - evaluate the idea on its own merits not the person who offers it.
- **Be punctual and honest**
- **Help the facilitator or teacher** do his job because it is yours.

Setting the stage

Seat the students in a circle or a hollow square - that everyone can see everyone else.

Provide the blackboard (or whiteboard) which everyone can see.

Arrange the material and audio-visuals in advance, if you plan to use and check them.

- Think about the dynamics of the group and anticipate problmes which may arise.
- Do not over-plan which may stifle the initiative and excitement.

The groups may be formed having 4 to 6 students each, who work together in 'buzz sessions' and each group makes a presentation in five to ten minutes relating to the issues and problems. One student from each group reports its findngs, which can be noted on a white sheet/blackboard. The advantage of this technique is that it enables you to get the views of the group rapidly and everyone gets a chance to talk in a few minutes. The students become more relaxed, involved and interested in the learning.

Solve all Problems

An exceptionally knowledgeable person with his deep knowledge of wide-ranging subjects has the capability to provide solutions to almost every problem. He has the intelligence required to undestand the basic nature of the problem and then work accordingly towards finding its solution. He always gives right advice to the right people at the right time. **—Sama Veda**

Rules of Participatory Learning

Individuals need inclusion, control and being effective. The person joins a group to achieve certain goals. When these are compatible with the group's goals, the group might be quite cohestive. In order that the group should be able to achieve its goals and to work well, the following needs and behaviours can be helpful.

Table : Tasks, Needs and Bahaviours in Group Learning

Tasks	Needs	Bahaviours
Task needs of the group for a clear goal for agreement about goal for plan of action, eh.	Must be met through Task Behaviour	Initiating Informing Clarifying Summarizing Consensus
Maintenance needs of the group for mutual support for clarity for mutual understanding	Must be met through maintenance behaviour	Harmonising Gate keeping Encouraging Compromising Giving feedback
Individual needs of the members : to belong to be respected for status for power for dependency, etc.	Must be met through group task and maintenance behaviour.	Aggressive behaviour Blocking Dominating Avoiding Abandoning

The individuals usually play the following roles accordingg to four-key factors; ideas, people, projects and direction in a group:

- *Ideas:* the 'Innovator' generates ideas and the 'Evaluator' checks them out.
- *People-oriented:* the 'Resource Investigator' has the outside contacts, whilst the 'Team Worker' concentrates on internal relations within the group.
- *Projects:* the 'Shaper' initiates projects whilst the 'Finisher' makes sure the group finishes what it starts.
- *Direction:* the 'Chair' guides the group's decision making and the 'Organiser' puts decisions into operation.

Group Behaviour

Most of us in real life work in a team, social or community context. This makes behaviour and relationships more crucial than the individual skills. Understanding and observing the behaviour of individual students in a group is critical so as to accentuate their positive roles, while improving the negative behaviour. The experts categorise the behaviours as given below:

Group Bahaviour Tasks and Conduct

1.	Initiating	Propose aims, idea, action or procedures
2.	Informing	Ask for or offer facts, ideas, feelings, or options
3.	Clarifying	Illuminate or build upon ideas or suggestions
4.	Summarizing	Pull data together, so group may consider where it is
5.	Consensus	Explore whether group may be nearing a decision; prevent premature decision-making.

Group Maintenance Behaviour that helps the group function productively:

1.	Harmonizing	Reconcile disagreements, relieve tension, help people explore differences
2.	Gate keeping	Bring others in, suggest facilitating procedures, keep communication channels open
3.	Encouraging	Be warm and responsive; indicate with words or facial expression that the contributions of others are accepted
4.	Compromising	Modify own positions so that group may move ahead; admit error
5.	Giving feedback	Tell others in helpful ways, how their behaviour is received.

Personal or Self-oriented Behaviour Conduct that interferes with the work of the group

1.	Aggressive behaviour	Attacks, deflates, uses sarcasm

2. Blocking	Resists beyond reason, uses 'hidden agenda' items which prevent group movement
3. Dominating	Interrupts, asserts authority, over-participates to point of interfering with others' participation
4. Avoiding	Prevents group from facing controversy; stays off subject to avoid commitment
5. Abandoning	Makes an obvious display of lack of involvement.

We spend our lives in groups of various sorts - the family, gang, team, work group, etc., but how often do we take the time to stop and observe what is going on in the group, or why its members are behaving in the way they are? Beter observation of behaviour helps to develop understanding and skills for better organisation.

Content versus Process

When we observe what the group is talking about, we are focussing on content. When we try to observe how the group is handling its communication, *i.e.,* who talks, how much or who talks to whom, we are focussing on process. Most topics emphasise the content—"what is good leadership", "how can I motivate my subordinates," "how can we make meetings more effective." They concern issues which are "there and then" in the sense of being abstract, future - or past-oriented, and not involving us directly. In focussing on group process, we are looking at what one group is doing in the "here and now", how it is working in the sense of its present procedures and organisation.

The content of conversations may often be the best clue as to what process issue may be on people's minds, particularly when they find it difficult to confront the issue directly. The person *who keeps* talking about the past, for example, may be indicating that he is unsure of the present. For him the past provides a refuge.

The process means to focus on *what* is going on in the group and dying to understand it in terms of other things that have gone on in the group. If we can observe and understand better the importance of process in group functioning, it should be possible for each one of us to make more appropriate contributions to improving or maintaining the efficiency and effectiveness of the groups to which we belong.

Communication

One of the easiest aspects of group process is to observe is the pattern of communication, which may be non-verbal or verbal:

- Who talks? for how long? How often?
- Whom do people look at when they talk?
  - (*a*) other individuals, possibly potential supporters
  - (*b*) the group
  - (*c*) no one
- Who talks after whom, or who interupts whom?
- What style of communication is used by group members (assertions, questions, tone of voice, gestures, etc.)?
- The kinds of observations we make in these process areas give us clues to other important things which may be going on in the group, such as who leads whom, who influences whom, who trusts whom, who supports whom, etc.

Decision-making Procedure

Whether we are aware or not, groups are making decisions all the time. Some of these decisions will be made consciously and in reference to the major tasks which the group has been set up to achieve. Some of them will, however, be made without much awareness or concern for these tasks but in response to the ways of behaving which have been established in the group. Often these will not be stated or written down but nevertheless they will be binding on group members and may even prevent formal group tasks from being undertaken. It is important to observe how decisions are made in a group order to assess the appropriateness of the decision to the matter being decided on, and whether the consequences of given methods are really what group members bargained for.

Group decisions are notoriously hard to undo. When someone says, "Well, we decided to do it, didn't we?" any budding opposition is quickly immobilized. We can only undo the decision if we reconstruct it to understand how we made it and test out whether this method was appropriate or not.

The procedure by which decision is taken will affect the effectiveness of the decision. The likelihood that the decision will be carried through as decided and with commitment - both of these conditions are important.

Some methods by which groups make decisions:

- The Plop: "I think we should introduce ourselves", followed by silence.
- The Self-authorized Agenda: "I think we should introduce ourselves, my name is Ram."
- The Handclasp: "I wonder if it would be helpful if we introduced ourselves? "I think it would, my name is Shyam Prasad". Does anyone object?" or "we all agree".
- Majority-Minority voting.
- Polling: "let's see where everyone stands, what do you think?"
- *Consensus Testing:* Genuine exploration to test for opposition and to determine whether opposition feels strongly enough not to be willing to implement decision; not necessarily unanimity, but essential agreement by all.

The above methods are not in any order of importance or usefulness. The effectiveness of any decision will depend on a number of factors including the significance of the matter to be decided on, the extent to which people want, need or are able to participate, and whether the emotions involved in the decision have been expressed, recognised and taken into account.

Self-oriented Behaviour

Behaviour in a group can be viewed from the point of view of what its purpose or function seems to be. When a member says or does something, is he primarily trying to get the group task accomplished (task), *or* is he trying to imporve or patch up some relationships among members (maintenance), or is he primarily meeting some personal need or goal without regard to the group's problems (self-oriented)? What kinds of categories can we identify?

Types of Behaviour Relevant to Group Learning

1. Initiating: Proposing tasks or goals; defining a group problem, suggesting a procedure or ideas for solving a problem.
2. Seeking information or opinions: Requesting facts, seeking relevant information about group concern; asking for expressions of feeling; requesting a statement or estimate; soliciting expressions of value; seeking suggestions and ideas.
3. Giving information or opinions: Offering facts; providing relevant information about group concern; stating opinions or beliefs about a matter before the group; giving suggestions and ideas.
4. Clarifying and Elaborating: Interpreting ideas or suggestions; clearing up of confusion; defining terms; indicating alternatives and issues before the group.
5. Summarizing: Pulling together related ideas; restating suggestions after the group has discussed them; offering a decision or conclusion for the group to accept or reject.
6. Seeking Decision: Testing for readiness to make decision; seeking decision-making procedure.
7. Taking Decision: Stating group's feelings in terms of a group decision; invoking the decision-making procedure.

For the group to be in good working order, it requires a good climate for task work, and good relationships which permit maximum use of member resources, *i.e.* group maintenance:

1. Harmonizing: Attempting to reconcile disagreements; reducing tension; getting people to explore differences.
2. Gate Keeping: Helping to keep communication channels open; facilitating the participation of others; suggesting procedures or processes that will sharing remarks.
3. Encouraging: Being friendly, warm, and responsive to others; indicating by facial expression or remark the acceptance of others' contributions.
4. Compromising: When own idea or status is involved in a conflict, offering a compromise which yields status; admitting error; modifying in interest of group cohesion or growth.
5. Standard Setting and Testing: Testing whether group is satisfied with its procedures or suggesting procedures; pointing out explicit or implicit norms which have been set to make them available for testing.

Every group needs both kinds of behaviour and work out an adequate balance of task and maintenance activities.

Emotional Issues

The group learning process attempts to solve problems of task and maintenance. However, there are many forces active in groups which distrub work, and which represent a kind of emotional underworld or undercurrent in the stream of group life. These underlying emotional issues produce a variety of behaviours which interfere with or are destructive of effective group functioning. However, they cannot be ignored or wished away. Rather, they must be recognised, their causes must be understood and, as the group develops, conditions must be created which permit these same emotional energies to be channelled in the direction of group effort.

The following are the types of behaviour which do not help the group learning but which represent an attempt on the part of an individual to meet some personal goal of his own, at the expense of or without regard for group goals:

1. Dominating: tyring to assert authority or superiority in manipulating the group, or certain members of it.
2. Blocking/difficulty stating: rejecting and discouraging group ideas and suggestions; stubbornness beyond "reason"; placing a difficulty or block in the path of a proposal or idea without offering a reasoned statement of disagreement.
3. Defending/attacking: attacking another person or defensively strengthening one's own position. (Defending/attacking behaviours usually involve overt value judgements and often contain emotional overtones).
4. Recognition, help or attention seeking: calling attention to oneself in various ways; "playboying"; attempting to call forth sympathy response through expressions of insecurity; personal confusion; depreciating oneself beyond reasonable limits.
5. Pairing up: seeking out one or two supporters and forming a kind of emotional sub-group in which the members protect and support each other.
6. Special interest pleading: speaking for particular interests (*e.g.* 'engineers', 'personal', management') as a cover for prejudice or stereotypes which best fit the individual's needs and desires.
7. Withdrawing: trying to remove the sources of uncomfortable feelings by psychologically leaving the group.

Those kinds of self-oriented behaviour arise because the individual, might be having certain problems, as given below:

1. The problem of identity and acceptance: Who am I in the group? Am I accepted here? Do I accept the other group members? What kind of behaviour is acceptable in this group? What do people expect of me?

2. The problem of goals and needs: What do I want from this group? Can the goals of the group be made consistent with my own goals? What have I to offer to the group?
3. The problem of power, control and influence: Who will control what we do? How much direction do I expect? How much power and influence do I have?
4. The problem of informaiton and intimacy: What do I know about the group and its members? What do they know about me? What do I want them to know about me? How close will we get to each other? How personal? How much can we trust each other and how can we achieve a greater level of trust?

Table: Verbal and Non-verbal Elements of Assertion

	Non-assertive	Assertive	Aggressive
Verbal	Apologies Dismiss own needs ("it's not important really") Self put downs ('I'm useless at . . .") Frequent justifications Few 'I' statements Qualifiers (just, sort of . . .) Nagaters	Statements clear, brief and to the point 'I' statements Distinction fact and opinion Suggestions not weighted with advice No 'shoulds' and 'oughts' Constructive criticism Questions to get facts Looking for solutions	Excess 'I' statements Boastfulness Possessiveness - 'my' Opinions and facts confused Threatening questions Reguests or instructions Sarcasm put downs
Non-Verbal	Wobbly voice Quiet voice, drops away Hesitent Frequent throat clearing Evasive look Looking down Hand over mouth Hunched shoulders Hand wringing Crossed, protective arms	Steady, firm voice Neither loud nor soft voice Modulated tone Fluent Steady pace Open reaction - smiles when pleased - frowns when angry Firm gaze Open movements Head erect Relaxed	Very firm tone Cold/sarcastic Strident/oud voice Fluent Abrupt Fast Scowls Chin forward Stares other down Finger pointing Fist thumping Arms crossed (unapproachable)

Source: Author's notes at training at School of Public Policy, University of Birmingham.

These issues are not the only kinds of things which can be observed in a group. What is important to observe will vary with what the group is doing, the needs of the observer and his purpose and many other factors. The main point is that imporving our skills in observing what is going on in groups should provide us with important data for understanding groups and increasing our effectiveness in and with them. In other words, if we cannot see what is going on in a group, our chances of behaving appropriately in that group are significantly reduced, however skilful we may be in communication.

Individual Characteristics

The individual characteristics and talents can be broadly fitted into the following eight roles:

Innovator: Groups and organisations need people with ideas. What distinguishes invovators is the volume and radical nature of the ideas they propose. They are individualistic and cleaver but may need careful handling to provide the vital spark.

Resource investigator: The Resource Investigator brings information and ideas to the team, but from sources outside the group. Friendly and gregarious with masses of contacts, they prevent the group stagnating, but can be lazy unless working under pressure.

Chair: The Chair is the social leader of the group the skill lies in spotting what each member does best and in guiding the team towards success. Commanding and decisive when the group needs to make a decision, but not domineering, they are quick to see unusual talent and able to get the best out of team members.

Shaper: The Shaper provides the energy and drive to implement the ideas and get projects moving. Dynamic, but possibly abrasive to people outside the group, they make good team leaders in growing organisations or active project groups.

Evaluator: The Evaluator critically appraises proposals, monitors progress and prevents the group making mistakes. Clever and dispassionate, they like time to mull things over and may appear cold and uncommitted, but are hardly ever wrong.

Team Worker: The Team Worker unites by providing an informal network of communication and support which continues outside meetings. They act as unofficial team leaders without whose presence the group might feud and fragment.

Organiser: They translale plans into manageable tasks. Disciplined, conscientious and methodical, they work for, and identify with the organisation, being practical and orthodox, but need to guard against inflexibility.

Finisher: The Finisher makes sure that the group delivers. Both a perfectionist and a compulsive meeter of deadlines, the finisher worries about what can go wrong and maintains a permanent sense of urgency which communicates itself to the group.

The purpose of participatory learning is not to label the individuals, but to accentuate positive roles which any individual can play in a group towards a synergy of active thinking and performance. Every individual, howsoever brilliant, can have some shortcomings, which could be identified for improvement.

> Newton's fourth law of exams:
>
> Every book will continue to be at rest, or covered with dust, until some external or internal exam moves it.'

CHAPTER 4

World-Class Education

"The world is ready to give up its secrets, if we only know how to knock, how to give the necessary blow. The strength and force of the blow comes through concentration." **—Swami Vivekananda**

Some basic changes in the existing methods of education are necessary in designing a world class education system. As education methods advance, it needs a break through from the traditional classroom mind-set, along with the following:

1. Plan the inputs to learning and education meticulously.
2. Don't use education professionals, depend more on practitioners.
3. Use mutual learning, not the traditional teacher-student roles.
4. Create opportunity for self and life-long learning.
5. Create environmental influences for learning.
6. Create institutional support structures.
7. Focus on students than the teachers, replace teaching by learning.

All but the most specialized topics in world-class universities are taught by world class institutes do not rely on regular teachers, but move on the facilitators and trainers who have performed. A misconception is that teacher must have professional qualifications in education. This further divides teacher and learner, professional teacher and consultant, teacher and doer, a division that has proven ineffective. All must teach and learn. As the Japanese say, "All teach". Students learn better from a teacher with field experience and personal practice in what is taught. It also provides a reality check on the curriculum.

Use mutual learning, not the traditional teacher-student roles: The traditional image of the teacher is one of a "master" who imparts wisdom by talking to students. This image belies the kind of learning happening within modern organizations. No teacher comes anywhere close to "knowing it all". Today the students are quite mature. A model of learning that recognizes these fact can be called mutual learning, in which a community or group of people share what each has learned and learn from others.

An environment for mutual learning is necessary even in the classroom, and many ways exist to create one. Homework can be posted on the wall so that the students can study each others' efforts, strong and weak. An example is using a workshop to "retrofit" problem they've solved and present them in a workshop. The participants discuss each other's work and formulate guidelines to improve probelm solving. This mutual learning format eliminates the need for teacher omniscience.

Mutual learning extends learning beyond the classroom if work groups rather than individuals can be trained together. Such training promotes a common language and teamwork and makes it easier to implement the results. People in teams teach each other better practices.

Presentations diffuse success stories. Exchange visits with work, groups, or companies provide opportunities for mutual learning and knowledge of the process. This is the great strength of mutual learning.

Organizational learning begins with personal learning and ultimately applies at all levels and every student. People resist improvement efforts. It requires going through the uncomfortable, awkward and perhaps risky or scary phases of conscious incompetence and conscious competence. Gaining skill requires commitment to three things: openness to learning, serious application, and mutual learning. The first step is willingness to learn, and even before that the willingness to admit you don't know. Several attitudes block openness to learning, which the students (including the teachers) have to give up. Knowing something is quite different both from having exposure to information and from possessing actual skill. It must not turn out informtion and abandon the acquisition of skills. Rules of thumb are not sufficient for long-term success in the real, complex world. However, these rules of thumb do allow us to begin to perform at a rudimentary level. With experience at rudimentary performance and with further study, we have a chance to improve our level of skill. In time, with enough experience and study, we can learn exceptions to the rules of thumb, sets of rules of thumb to cover different situations, and an intuitive feel for what needs to be done in particular situations.

Skill development moves from conscious, usually awkward, application of rules of thumb, through conscious but increasingly fluid performance, and ultimately to an unconscious ability to handle myriad specific situations well. The fundametnal issue of skill development is "reflective practice" on what one learned, and practising it. It comprises a structured learning which integrates various skills and resources.

Improvised Performance

In practically every instance, what we take for creativity is actually inspired application of hard-won skill. The renowned dancer/choreographer Martha Graham put it this way: "Technique is the craft which underlies creativity." In many fields - music, language study, debate, acting, dance-improvised performance is practised until it comes easily, often through a combination of fragments of practised routines.

Inspiration from Masters

Serious students typically study with masters, or at least study the methods of masters, to learn the tradition and best current practice. Accomplished musicians and dancers tell who their teachers were and their teachers' teachers. Accomplished baseball and basketball players can explain whose swing or shot they copied. World champion sailboat racer Dennis Connor says to copy the methods of the fastest sailboat racers in your class and get going as fast as they can go before developing your own improvements.

Mastering a Skill

There are typically a variety of different methods or schools for teaching the same fundamental skills, or emphasizing different aspects of them, for instance, techniques in modern dance. Even at high levels of mastery, coaches are available who objectively watch for breaks in form or weak skills. If such coaching is not available, practitioners often develop methods of self-coaching whereby they objectively look at their own performance.

In the course of developing high skill levels, students frequently work their way through various positions, learning the skill from all perspectives and understanding the total picture, or they make significant changes in their game strategy as their skill improves. In sailboat racing, one may start by repacking sails in the bowels of the boat, get promoted to trimming a sail, increase ability to calling tactics, and finally end up skippering a boat.

The Myth of Talent and Luck

Superior performance has little to do with luck. In the long and short run, the non-master is simply no match for a master; neither is the less skilled person a match for the more skilled person on average.

Individual mastery is the key to competitive performance and is inevitably an acquired capability; for all practical purposes, even the person with the most natural talent is not born with mastery but rather has to acquire it through extended effort.

We are not talking about what is required to become world champion in a field, but about a level equivalent to shooting par on a golf course, to playing even with the teaching pro at a local tennis club, or to learning a new dance and performing it competently. Many people without so-called natural talent achieve this level of skill we call mastery.

David Walden talks of his following experience:

"When I first got out of college and went to work at MIT Lincoln Laboratory, I was assigned not to a project but to a senior engineer who was assigned to the project. I was his to use and teach. Soon, offices were rearranged so that I shared half of a two-person office with my mentor. I went everywhere with him. He would break off little pieces of design or implementation (a day or two long) and give them to me to do. We talked through "our" design and implemenation together, he answered my questions about why we were doing this or that and he gently helped me see problem and improvement in what I had done. And he praised me for how quickly I did my little bits and how quickly I caught on (whether or not it was completely justified).

After a month or two, I was doing bigger pieces, but because we shared an office, my mentor knew when I was struggling and would talk to me about what I was working on. Also, he would ask me to look over what he had done and give him comments. Since he was responsible for system integration in addition to developing some of the system modules, in time I became the second most knowledgeable person about the whole project. After a year or so, I began to receive more independent assignments, but we still shared the office and he never stopped being my teacher, though I had become his co-worker rather than trainee."

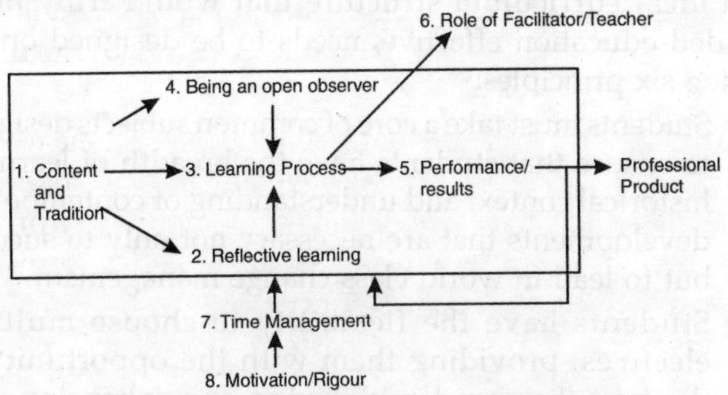

Eight Steps towards Achieving Mastery

Source: Adapted from Shiba, Shoji and David Wallace, 1993, Four Practical Revolutions in Management.

Embedded Learning

> The grace of the guru is like an ocean. If one comes with a cup he will only get a cupful. It is no use complaining of the niggardliness of the ocean. The bigger the vessel the more one will be able to carry. It is entirely up to him. —**Ramana Maharshi**

Embedded learning is a contemporary educational term and its interpretation varies with different users. In fact, this term represents integrated interdisciplinary learning in the context of the role of technology in education. The inter-disciplinry focus prepares students not only to specialise in specific areas, but also to develop a broad-based learning foundation.

Embedded education is not only discipline-centred, but also problem-centred education to engage and involve students. Integration of knowledge from various disciplines, conversion of learning into innovations, commercialisation of innovations and fostering a culture of entrepreneurship are important pillars of embedded education.

An embedded curriculum places more emphasis on experiential learning. It replaces the traditional model of 'learn-and-then-do' with a newer 'learning-while-doing' model. Professional ethics is also embedded in the curriculum.

An ideal curriculum structure that would truly make embedded education effective, needs to be designed on the following six principles:

- Students must take a core of common subjects designed to ensure that students have the breadth of learning, historical context and understanding of contemporary developments that are necessary not only to succeed but to lead in world class change management.
- Students have the flexibility to choose multiple electives, providing them with the opportunity to discover their academic passion and enhancing their engagement in the learning process through individualisation of their programmes of study.
- Students specialise in subject areas of their choice.
- Courses with an international focus in their programmes of study.
- Students are trained in and participate in real, experiential and applied learning.
- Students take courses to prepare them for a life-long commitment to leadership grounded in values, ethics and service to society.

In embedded learning the role of the teacher changes dramatically. No longer the keeper of knowledge and an academic, he is an interpreter of information guiding students through the mass of facts and data online and facilitating them how to discern quality from rubbish.

New Generation Technology

Education is acquiring a new dimension in view of the new generation that is intrinsically digital. ICT is one of the latest technology tools, which is a great enabler and drives the quality of education provided by an educational institution. Technology, while spearheading a revolution in the sphere of education, has also posed a unique challenge. The biggest challenge that we face today is to create more open resources for a better learning process.

Innovation is not just about introducing new, high-tech products. Joseph Schumpeter, a pioneering innovation economist, defined innovation as the recognition of opportunities for profitable change, and the pursuit of those opportunities all the way through to their adoption in parctice. It means that innovation is a broad concept.

It is not just about creating new products or services, but about 'change.' It, therefore, includes new ways of doing things, such as the assembly line or the direct sale of PC, new services such as online banking or micro-credit, or new business models such as low-cost flying or free newspapers.

Entrepreneurs drive that process by creating new products, new firms and new markets. They transform ideas, or technologies, into social artefacts. Often, entrepreneurs also drive scientific progress. Entrepreneurial cultures that exist without a scientific environment tend to get stuck into no-growth ventures. Increasingly, developing basic science must go hand-in-hand with developing the entrepreneural culture.

As part of its 'Mobile for Good' programme and its strategic focus on education in India, the Vodafone Foundation in collaboration with Pratham Education Foundation, announced its commitment to provide learning solution for over 50,000 underprivileged children across India. Vodafone Foundation has committed ₹ 140 million to provide the 'Learning with Vodafone Solution' across 1000 schools in India. A successful pilot project has been conducted in schools across Karnataka and Vodafone Foundation looks at building on this and replicating the same success in Tamil Nadu, Maharashtra and Delhi. The solution offers digital educational content aligned to the prescribed curriculum, SMS multiple choice tests, etc.

Technology Platforms and Open Ended Learning (OELE)

A key element of Open Technology Platform is the Learning Management System (LMS). It is an enterprise level learning management solution for Open-ended learning system; it provides a holistic learning experience to the students, collaborative knowledge sharing experience for the teachers and students and operational efficiency to the administrators. Using the technology teachers can stream-line processes, track student performance and deliver a consistent training message to the user's desktop. It allows students to learn at their own pace and have continual feedback on the progress of their education. Learning is breaking out of the narrrow boxes. There is an increasing dialogue in global education circles towards student centred learning. Open eneded learning may take many different forms in terms of student behaviour and learning goals:

1. **Problem-based Learning:** The students may be inducted into a certain context of a problem and may be taken through a set of learning activities in order to be able to solve specific problems.
2. **Inquiry-based Learning:** Students may seek to delve deeper into specific challenges in the subject area and may seek to pursue answers to specific questions that they may encounter in the course of their learning.
3. **Case-based Learning:** Students may work on cases with definite context having a set of questions to work on and may arrive at set of alternaives for solutions.
4. **Discovery-based Learning:** The students may follow an organic path of discovery in their learning and may explore continously into their areas of interest leading to research and formulation of hypothesis.
5. **Social Learning:** Students may engage in more informal modes of learning involving extensive interactions among their communites and group and may validate their views by sharing with similar minded students.

The OELEs may be pursued on multiple technology platforms that are now available. These platforms may fall into three categories:

- Open and free platforms where anyone interested may join and participate.

- Available by specific invitation and subscriptions and moderated groups.
- University related and having goals associated with degrees and certifications.

Social Learning

The modern student is SMART - Systematic, Meticulous, Active, Realistic and Tactful. Albert Bandrura, Professor of Psychology at the Standford University has put forth a Theory of Social Learning. It says that the most learning takes place due to observation and imitation. This 'observational learning' was empirically confirmed in Bandura's famous Bobo doll experiment of 1961, wherein children who watched adults being violent towards dolls later replicated the same behaviour without any inducement or provocation.

While it would be a stretch to link the observational models of learning (that rely more on physical proximity and observations) to the social media tools of today, it would be difficult to totally disregard the important role social media plays in helping discover and connect with people or follow conversations that one might never have come across in the physical world. By enlarging and enriching the universe from which one can draw upon for experiences and acquaintances, social media is doing yeoman's service in expanding learning.

Social media has had a profound impact on politics. Barack Obama raised millions of dollars in campaign funding through twitter. Social media has had a great impact on governance campaigns such as India Against Corruption. Social media has impacted almost all areas of human endeavour.

A study at the Purdue University established that use of Twitter in the classroom helped students overcome the shyness barrier, by allowing them to answer questions without having to raise hands to identify themselves in a big lecture hall. Increased participation, in turn, has been linked to better academic performance. Increased communication also opens up perspectives and allows one to appreciate different points of view.

Tools such as Twitter allow classrooms to transcend limitations imposed by physical space, costs involved in increasing capacity and challenges of holding attention of a large audience. With increasing smartphone and tablet penetration, Twitter integration with classroom teaching has become feasible.

A number of 'real world' courses make significant use of Second Life. Instructors develop simulations in the virtual world that aid experiential and immersive learning. For example, history courses have Second Life tour of the places and events being taught in a geography class is brought alive with simulated tours. Engineering students can build simulated versions of buildings, tools, machines, robots, solar energy, etc. and see for themselves how the theory plays out in reality. Virtual meeting halls allow student and faculty to interact and plan out the schedule.

Good teaching is about style. Good teaching should also be entertaining.

Intel's Model for Education Transformation

- **Policy:** Policies designed to ensure that all students obtain the skills necessary to succeed in a knowledge-based economy and society, are of key importance for the society and the students to remain globally competitive.
- **Curriculum Standards and Assessment:** Curriculum standards must be adapted to ensure students learn the critical skills and knowledge to succeed in the global economy. We need to have in place the system that can conduct robust assessment of a student's knowledge and skills.
- **Professional Development:** Teacher's need to change their method of teaching for creating a student-centred learning environment. New teaching methods, such as

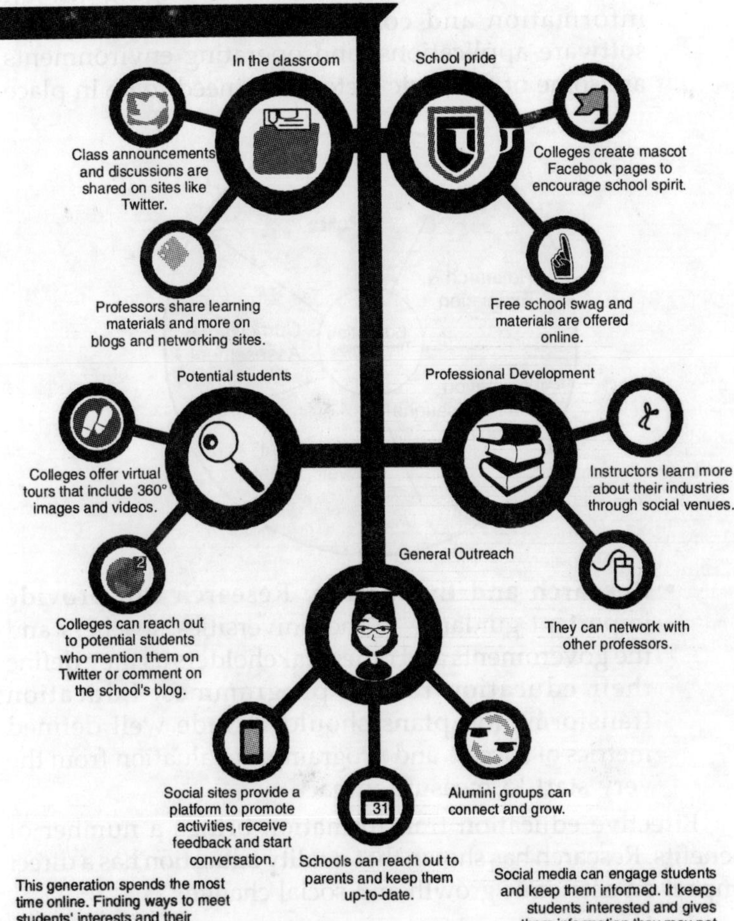

Source: www.digitallearning.ingraphics-mashable

inquiry and project-based approaches, should be used. Teachers need tools and training to adjust their pedagogic approaches to take advantage of a transformed learning environment and available technology tools.

- **Information and Communications Technology (ICT):** ICT is an essential foundation for a transformed learning environment. Broadband internet connectivity, infrastructure for managing student information and content resources, appropriate software applications, and operating environments, are some of the basic factors that need to be in place.

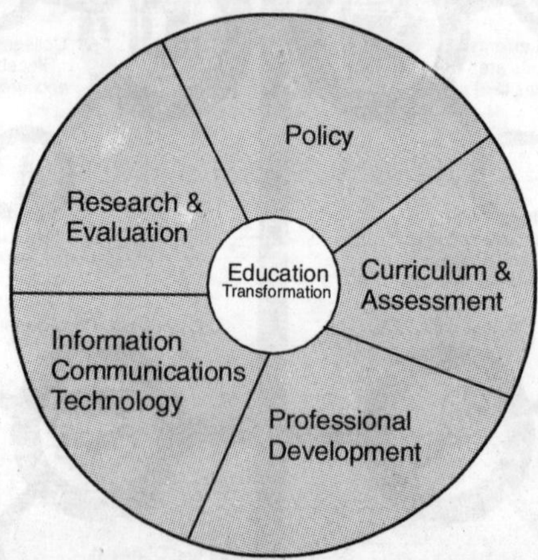

- **Research and Evaluation:** Research can provide important guidance to the universities, teachers and the governments and other stakeholders as they define their education reform programmes. Education transformation plans should include well defined metrics of success and programme evaluation from the very start to measure impact.

Effective education transformation brings a number of benefits. Research has shown that quality education has a direct impact on economic growth and social change :

- Increasing student competitiveness by developing skills such as digital literacy, problem solving, critical thinking and collabortion.
- Helping citizens develope lifelong learning skills, and better preparing them for current and future employment.
- Creating economic development as local businesses benefit from a better-educated citizenry and workforce.

- Creating more social cohesion and a better social climate as access to technology, the internet and digital content narrows the digital divide and creates opportunities.
- Immediate economic benefits to local businesses that help develope and deliver education solutions.

Education transformation has a huge impact on the society in creating economic and social opportunities for all. Intel works with governments to improve the quality of education system.

Source: digitalLEARNING, December 2011.

Lateral Thinking

Edward de Bono, author of more than 60 books, developed the concept of lateral thinking. He taught the subject in universities like Oxford, Cambridge, Harvard and delivered talks amongst a host of Nobel laureates.

Bono has developed a five-stage process or framework of thinking - TO, LO, PO, SO and GO. TO refers to where we are going, or the aims, objectives and the purpose of thinking which determine the direction of thinking. LO involves looking into the information needed, available and accumulation of the same. PO refers to the stage of generating every alternative possibility and solution. SO involves selection of the best from the available alternatives. Finally GO involves going ahead or action teps. Evidently the emphasis is more on perception and information from which decisions flow.

Edward de Bono has put forward a number of techniques to help people structure their thinking processes. He called this lateral thinking and his *Six Thinking Hats* is one example. Each hat represents a different way in which a topic could be discussed, as follows:

White Hat

White suggests paper. The white hat concerns information. When we consciously put on the white hat we ask ourselves questions like: "What information do we have?"; "What information do we need?"; "What questions should we be asking?". The white hat draws our attention to what we know and what we do not know.

Green Hat

Green suggests energy and life. The green hat is for creativity and new ideas. When we wear our green hat we try to be as creative as we can.

Grey Hat

Grey suggests authority and judgement. The grey hat is for caution. When we adopt the grey hat we evaluate ideas to look for the weaknesses, limitations and dangers.

Lateral Thinking Exercise

1. Divide participants into pairs.
2. Ask one of the pair to select a conflict situation that he/she is knowledgeable about.
3. The other party then selects a 'hat' (other than 'blue') and within that mode put questions to the other participant. These questons should explore the 'underlyng motivations' which are driving one of the stakeholders in the conflict.
4. After ten minutes the questioner chooses a different 'hat' and carries on questioning. If time allows, the questioner continues working through the different 'hats'.
5. End the exercise with the 'blue' hat, which is about reflection and planning a way forward.
6. In plenary discuss the results and the relative utility of the different 'hats', which mode worked best and why?

Yellow Hat

Yellow suggests sunshine and optimism. The yellow hat stimulates us to look for the positive aspects of the matter in hand. When we are wearing the yellow hat we explore the benefits and advantages of an idea.

Red Hat

Red suggests fire and warmth. The red hat is to do with feelings, intuition and emotions. When we chose to put on the red hat we take an opportunity to explore our feelings about the matter.

Blue Hat

Blue suggests water and reflection. The blue hat is for managing the whole thinking process by reflecting on where we are, where we want to be and what we need to do next. When we chose the blue hat we are signalling a period of review and summary. It is not necessary to have to talk about coloured hats to think in a particular way. The 'hats' only suggest a particular type of approach to a negotiation and a way to formulate the right questions. Thus the outcome of thinking becomes a product of systematic process involving logical flow and requisite emotions.

Squares: Issue the squares handout (see diagram) to each participant and ask them to say how many squares they see. Ask them to explain how they came to that answer. After some time, it will be discovered that there are 30 squares in the grid and not 16 or so that they see more immediately. Debrief on why people perceive the same things differently and how to deal with that in a group process (UNICEF, 1998).

The answer to the "how many different squares" question is 30

16 of 1 small square each, as per grid
9 of 4 small squares each (2 × 2)
4 of 9 small squares each (3 × 3)
1 of 16 small squares each (4 × 4)

Nine dot problem: Issue the nine dot diagram to each participant and ask them to individually join all the dots with only four, straight, connected lines and without lifting the pen from the paper from the start of the pattern to the end. Walk around and check who has done it right. Then ask those who have the correct solution to explain to the others. If none has it right, explain the solution and display the complete figure yourself. Ask participants what made the exercise difficult, what assumptions they made and why they never thought of drawing outside the imaginary boundaries. Debrief on the lesson: that we often fail to get solutions to problems because we restrict our thinking to the known rather than exploring extended frontiers ("thinking outside the box") (UNICEF, 1996).

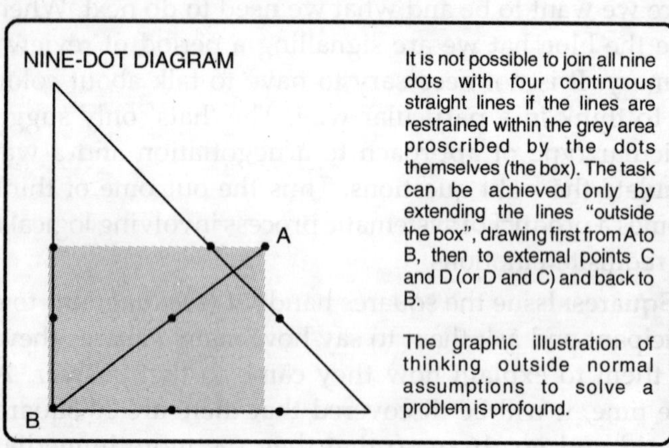

Source: Authoris notes during training at Overseas Development Institute.

CHAPTER 5

Personal Organisation

"Vision - is seeing the invisible, which reaches beyond the thing that is, into the conception of what it can be. Imagination gives you the picture, vision gives you the impulse to make the picture your own."

—Robert Collier

Being a university student is tough. He/She has to study many subjects, prepare for the examinations, submit the sessional work, besides many preoccuations and programmes, personal care, entertainment, friends and relations. There is a constant struggle and predicament what to do, what not to do. Some students give up in frustration, while some decide upon their priorities and resort to personnel organisation.

Personal Organisation is defined as a coherent and systematic approcah to life. An individual who is "personally organised" in this sense is always in a position to articulate his actions and the reasons for them. They organise themselves in order to maximise their personal effectiveness by matching their capacities to their actions in all spheres of their life. They can avoid becoming too busy or fatigued by astute selection of priorities. When immedite and unpredicted events occur they can respond immediately and appropriately. The are able to accommodate with minimum confusion the deadlines and schedules of longer-term projects. Typically, such an individual. "can ward off the alligators while working on plans to drain the swamp", perfectly balancing short- and long-term activities.

Techniques for "managing time" or "being organised" aim to serve this ideal. They comprise such obvious things as computer/mobile/diary/wall charts and filing cabinets.

Another element of personal organisation is the balance you maintain between activities that you are required to do by others and those which you initiate for yourself. These activities are often mutually supportive and add to your learning, recreation, hobbies and social activities. Personal organisation can help maintain the space and impetus for these self-motivated activities. An important element of personal organisation is the balance between reactive and proactive activity. Reactive activity involves actions you do in response to what your external world requires of you. This includes "fire-fighting", but may also include work whose urgency or necessity can be questioned. Personal organisation involves having systems and self-awareness that will help reduce ambiguity about what does and does not need to be done.

Education or Learning?

Education is what remains after one has forgotten everything be learned in school.

—Albert Einstein

Education or learning is nothing but organised thinking. The difference between an educated profesional and a layman is in their thought process. This is reflected in their communications, relationships, planning and actions. It is never too late to introspect and make a new beginning. The organised, creative thinking manifests the following sequence:

- Emptying, and removing clutter of information overload. Unconditioning of the mind makes it free from preconceived notions and prejudices.
- Listen, observe and search, collect relevant facts and figures.
- Understand, think, digest and focus.

- Think - why, what, where, how and when?
- Concentrate and aggregate, analyse and disaggregate.
- Synergise, synthesise, visualise the big picture.
- Exchange ideas and notes, communicate, interact, triangulate, crosscheck, debrief and discuss.
- Develop concepts and options, structure and process.
- Consolidate, refine, review, do detailing and experimentation.
- Application and translation of ideas into strategy and action.
- Output, feedback, relearning and reform.

Every student is faced with several problems and complexities in his/her studies and personal life. In a real world they find that the situation does not respond to the idealism - that this should be done and that should not be done. For any shortcomings and failures, it is easy to find the scapegoats. Lack of time is a common excuse. Helplessness towards politics is another general complaint. Usually the students and teachers are trained to deal with the problems of others. They are most happy to advice and manage the life of others, rather than for themselves. The conventional education is too often engrossed in discussing the failures and shortcomings of policies, progammes and education.

The students hardly realise that it is their own mindset which is the missing link between theory and practice, between norms and behaviour, between knowledge and performance and between input and output. As a result they often indulge in wishful thinking - what should be done rather than what can be done, how and when.

Learning entails understanding, carrying forward and tying up multiplicity of experiences, abilities and perceptions. This involves a realistic understanding of one's own role in a team or society and how best one can organise himself within the prevailing environment, which may not be of one's liking or choice. This is a complex task. One has to shed away rigidity and preconceptions about the people, procedures or situations. One has to be able to see the things as they are, sensitively observe the emotions and perceive the unwritten rules of operation. One has to understand the hidden issues beyond the visible, which include flow of information, speaking, timing and personal inter-relationships.

A Personal Action Plan (PAP) can be a vehicle to optimise learning and transmit learning into practice. If no improvement or change is reflected in the individual's performance, the purpose of learning, experience or training would be futile. The PAP cycle comprises the following:

1. Developing a positive attitude towards learning
2. Understanding
3. Observation
4. Experience/Contents
5. Distillation, Conceptualisation Analysis and Evolving a Process
6. Communication
7. Experimentation
8. Performance.

A Personal Action Plan involves synthesis of experiences, understanding, perceptions, learning and abilities into a workable plan for an individual. As such, a Personal Action Plan (PAP) translates and accomplishes learning into the practice. The objective of the PAP, is to draw up a realistic plan of action which can be implemented in particular context. Its contents consist of an analysis of the problem, identifying the main actors and the individual's role and place among them, statement of objectives, action and a programme. The process is to identify the options and relate these with concrete experience, reflective observations abstract conceptualisation and active experimentation. The UCLA has also developed a four step tool kit for the students to enhance their mental capabilities and optimise the learning :

Step 1 : Relabel a gien thought, feeling or behaviour as something else. This amounts to training yourself to clearly recognised and identify what is real and what isn't, refusing to be tricked by your own thoughts.

Step 2 : Reattribute. This answers the question, "Why do these thoughts keep coming back?' The answer is that the brain is misfiring, stuck in gear, creating mental noise, and sending false messages.

Step 3 : Refocus. This involves the actual changing of behaviour. You now have to replace he old behaviour with new things to do. This is where the change in brain chemistry occurs, because you are creating new patterns, new mindsets. By refusing to be misled by the old messages, by understanding they aren't what they tell you they are, your mind is now in charge of your brain.

Step 4 : Revalue. This is the natural outcome of the first three. With a consistent way to replace the old behaviour with the new, you begin to see old patterns as simple distractions. You devalue them as being completely worthless. Eventually the old thoughts begin to fade in intensity, the brain works better, and the automatic transmission in the brain begins to start working properly.

The emphasis is on developing a creative mind, as Albert Einstein said,

> 'the true sign of intelligence is not knowledge but imagination.'

> Training is everything.
> The peach was once a bitter
> almond; cauliflower is
> nothing but cabbage with
> a college education.
> **Mark Twain**

CHAPTER 6

Communicating Effectively

You never get a second chance to make a first impression.

—Anonymous

In this competitive world communication plays a vital part in learning and presenting the content and one's personality. It becomes quite essential to present right terms to express one's views or to answer a question. In communication, it is a profanity to use complicating and tortuous language. In a conversation, it is very important to acknowledge, establish information intent, bridge little gaps, ensure that the counterparts receive your message and are provoked to ask questions.

The key elements of learning is to understand how the human psyche works (UNICEF, 1998):

We learn	We remember
1% through taste	10% of what we read
2% through touch	20% of what we hear
3% through smell	30% of what we see
11% through hearing	50% of what we see and hear
83% through sight	80% of what we say
	90% of what we say and do

This implies 'What I hear, I forget, what I see I remember, what I do I do I know'. Tuckman (1965) defined the learning sequence in four words - forming, storming, norming and performing. In this guest communication tools become critical. As the above chart shows visuals are most effective tool of Harming (83%). The visuals can be in various forms graphics, photographs, models, charts, etc.

A presentation has to be easily digestible. It is important to define the purpose, analyse the audience, construct or develop the message with due estimate of time and length, decked on a most appropriate style and media for presentation. Develop a storyline, linking various segments of the topic. Your viewpoint is shaped by your views. Where you stand depends upon where you sit. By positioning key words in the opening lines, you can prepare the others to participate in the conversation. Some tips for this can be the following :

- Clarity about conversational intent makes it easier for another to react.
- Draw a big picture with clarity.
- Establish your role in conversation and streamline it into a channel that is aimed at.
- Insert your visual map about ideas into precise words in a conversation. Do not over-stress, over-explain the point.
- Bridge those little gaps that creep into a conversation.
- Do not overload the listener with data and complex technicalities. Not all data are informative, not all information comes from data. Not all information and data are important. Make sure the basis is solid before expanding it.
- Be brief, to the point, remember holding the attention of the audience, which becomes difficult after 10-15 minutes. Give relief by jokes, light anecdotes after every 10-15 minutes. Try to involve audience by

interactive talk. However, do not let the focus get blurred.

- Simplify the complex and also explain the complexities of simple. Each anecdote, diagrams/graphic, picture, visual and cartoon can convey what the speaker would otherwise explain in a thousand words.
- Know what you don't know and then take steps to get right information and expert assistance. Treat your audience with respect, do not feed them with rudimentary, hackneyed information, quotes or sermons. Certainly they are not school children and expect a mature, professional dialogue. Generally students and audience dislike too much "teaching".
- It takes more time to do things than you hope but less time than you think. Divide your time according to importance of the subject matter and emphasis, focusing upon the central purpose of the talk.
- Take principles of management with grains of salt. Treat trivialities trivially. Don't sweat the small stuff. Differentiate between important issues and matters. Respect the value of time of the listener, do not waste their time on marginal issues. A presentation should not convey the idea of giving a 'lecture'.

Be Clear

By conveying the message with clarity, we help others to visualize a clearer picture and evoke greater empathy. Adding specific directional cues to your words helps convey sincerity and involvement. This allows the message to transmit the emotions, feelings and intent of the communication better. Convey what you see or hear, "I read in the report of your---.'

- Add how you feel. 'I feel we ought to try out another route.'

- Add reason. 'Because I have seen this work in the past---'
- Speak out what you want 'What I now want is a new approach.'
- Mention the objective. 'So that we get to meet our targets'

Questions that require 'yes-no' responses generally kill the conversation. Open ended questions allow for more thought out and committed responses. A speaker should be articulate, but more important for him/her is to know where and when to stop:

"There was a man of great verbosity,
Who loved words of great ferocity,
Waxing profound,
He fell to the ground,
Knocked out by his own pomposity"

Graphic Tools

It is being realized that too verbose and hard mediums of communication are less effective than the soft mediums - graphics, metaphors, humour, etc. They are to be used appropriately and innovatively in education. They can have a surprise element that keep the listener absorbed and provoked.

Various graphic tools simplify the complex. These also save long, boring explanations and help to understand the linkages between various dimensions of an issue/hypothesis. The graphics should be simple which can be drawn on white board by the speaker/participant or drawn on computer for a power point presentation. The text on graphics should be minimum, brief and catchy - no sentences, only bullet points. The graphics and digarams can communicate the message in several ways combining hard and soft mediums.

Matrix data analysis

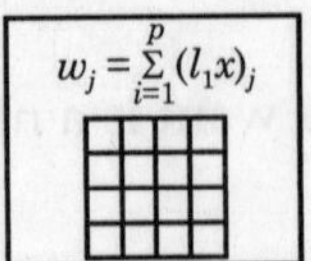

Matrix diagram

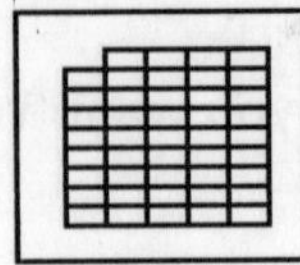

Stratification

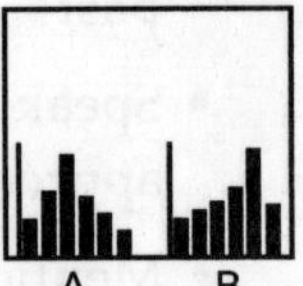

Pareto Diagram

Tree diagram

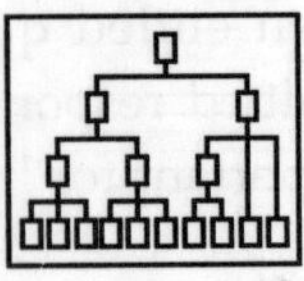

Control Chart

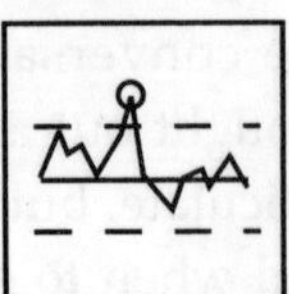

Cause-and-Effect Diagram

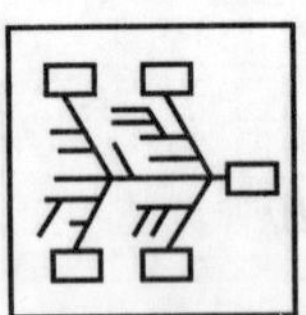

Check Sheet

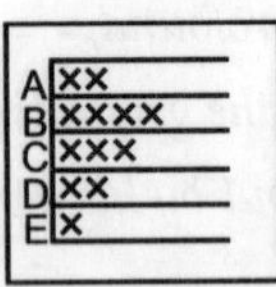

Histogram

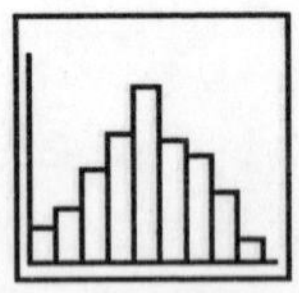

Relations diagram

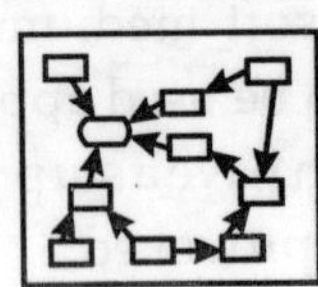

Scatter Diagram

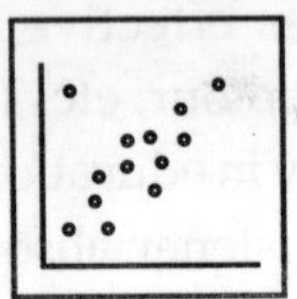

Graphs

Arrow diagram

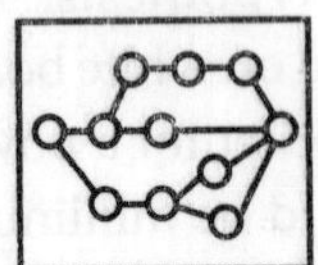

Affinity diagram

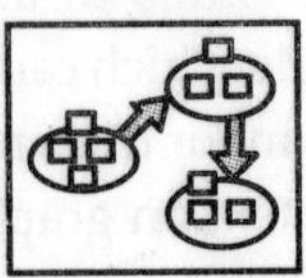

E2
E1 E3
E4

Various Types of Diagrams : Each Graphic explains what thousand words would otherwise do.

Various Types of Graphics

Message	Graphical Medium (Examples)
Position, Reality	Graph, Matrix chart, Histogram
Survey, Plan	Map
Problem	Control Chart, Scatter Diagram, Box Chart
Analysis	Arrow/Diamond Diagram
Specifics	Check sheet, stratification
Checklist	Check sheet
Process, Roadmap, Flow Diagram	Tree, Arrow, Pyramid, Flower, Sun diagram
Concept	Bubble, Triangle, Square, Hexagon, Circle, etc.
Metaphor	Geometric Chart
Comparison	Control Chart
Humour	Cartoon
Ambiguity, Paradox, Contradiction	Sketch/Cartoon
Generalisation, Classifcation	Spherical Segmented Chart
Connection, Linkages	Relation/Affinity/Arrow/Ladder Diagram
Difference, Breaks	Process Chart, Cycle, Circle, Shell, Spiral, Bicycle, etc.
Evaluation Assessment	Polygon/Matrix

Matrix Chart

Matrix Analysis

Issues		What	Who	How	Data	Observation	Abstraction	Application	Proxy	Triangulation	Interview
Service delivery	P										
	C										
Institutional/ managerial	P										
	C										
Financial	P										
	C										
Tech./ Env.	P										
	C										

P–Provider
C–Consumer

Project Management Matrix

Level \ Scale	Region/City	Sub-City Zone/ Sectoral	Local Area	Project
1. Policy				
2. Strategic				
3. Operational/ Action				

Stepped Matrix Chart

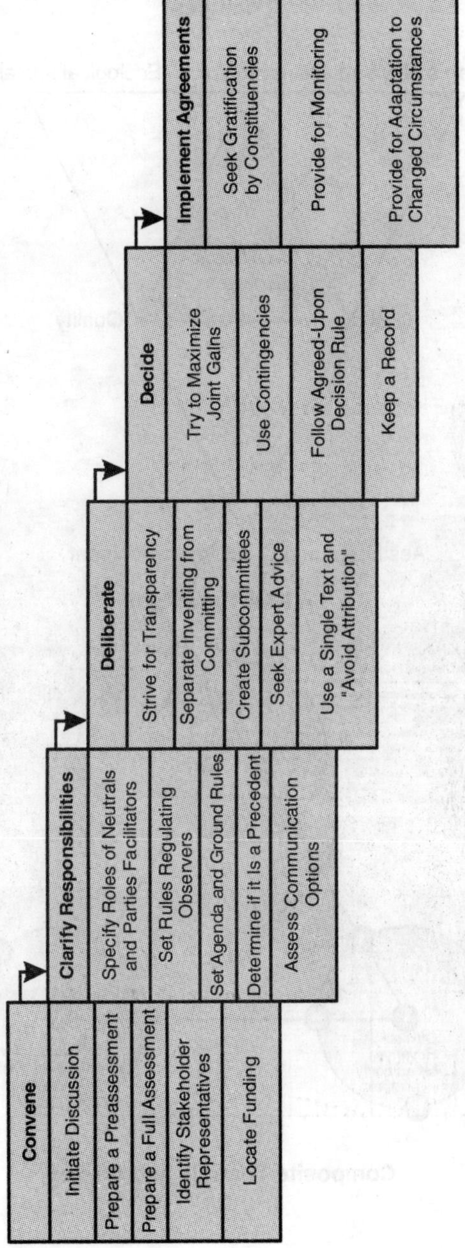

Triangles

A New Paradigm

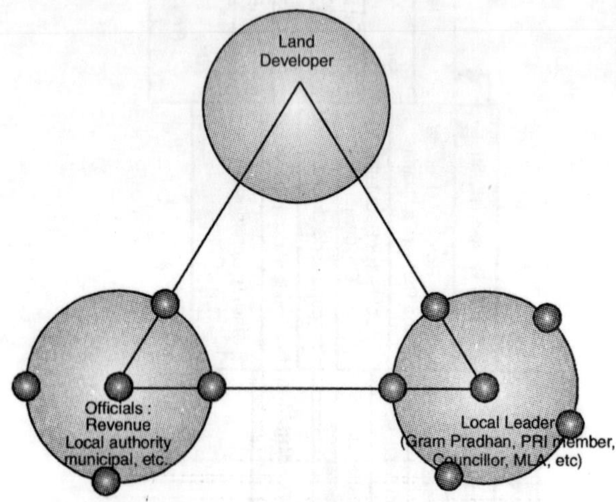

Composite Triangle and Circles

Pyramid Charts

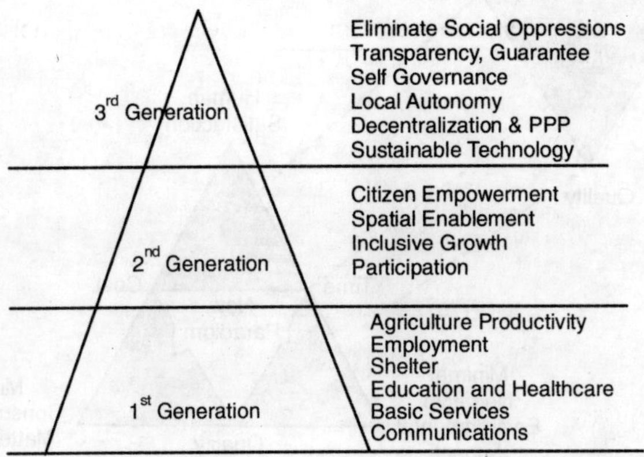

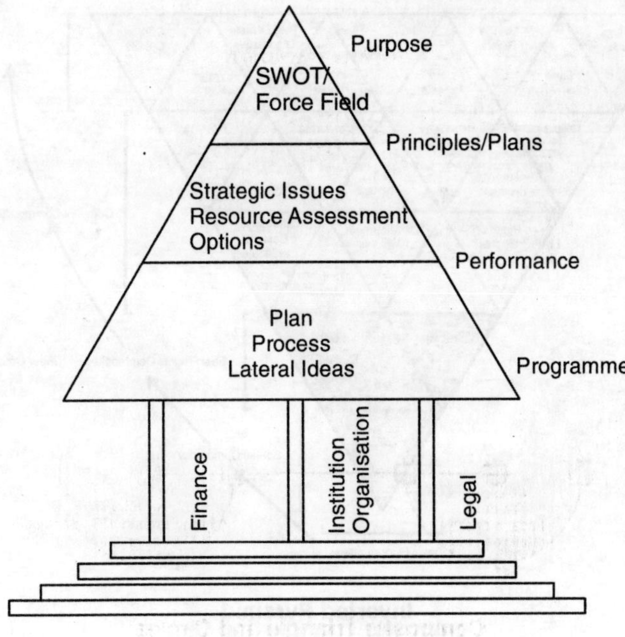

Project Planning Pyramid

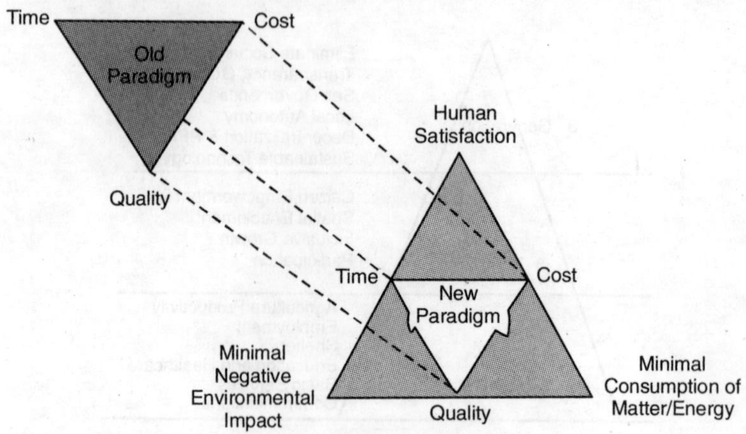

Old and New Paradigm

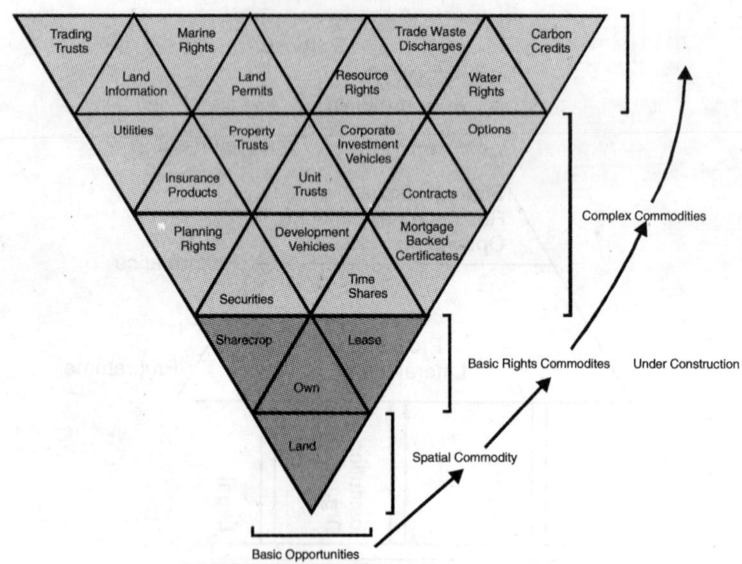

Inverted Pyramid

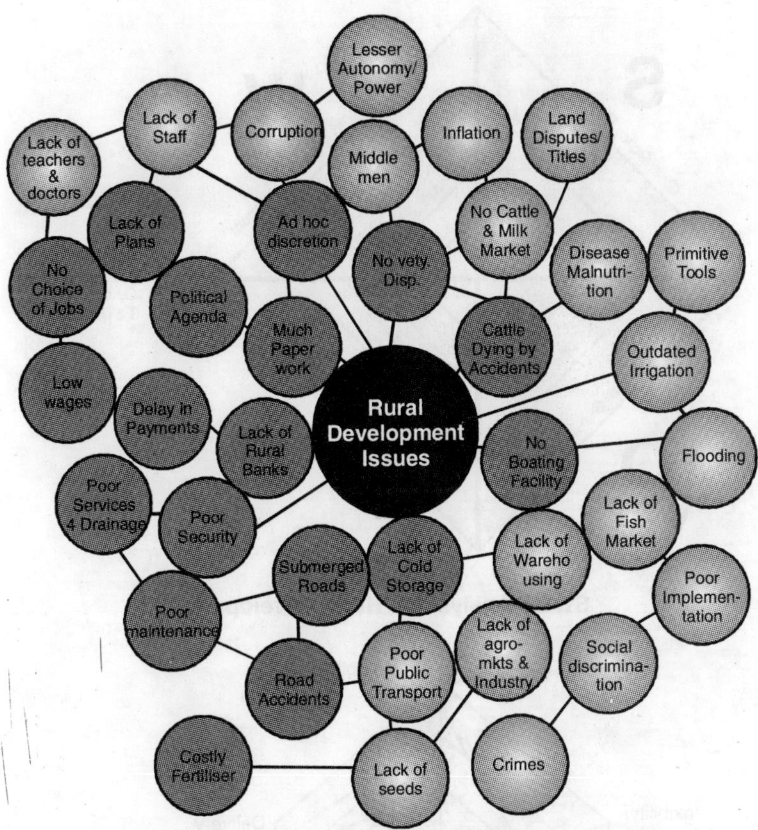

Balloon Chart Identifing Major Issues and Challenges of Rural Development

Diamond Chart

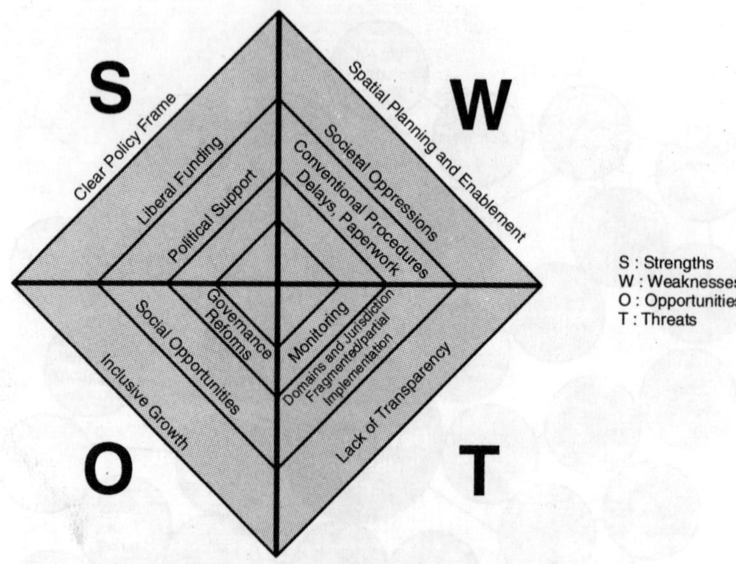

SWOT Analysis of Rural Development

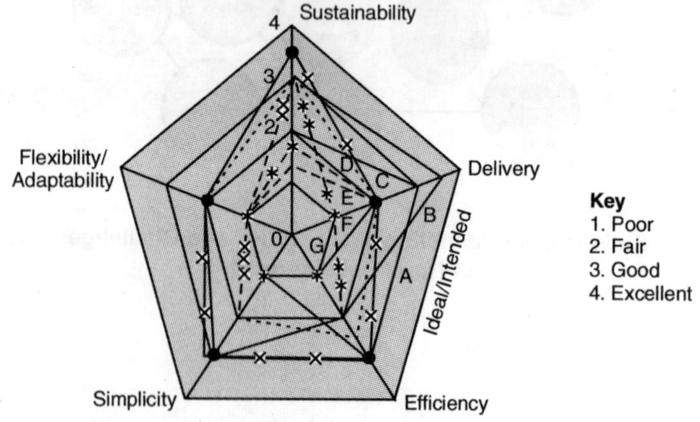

Rating of Key Components in Development Delivery

The Sphere

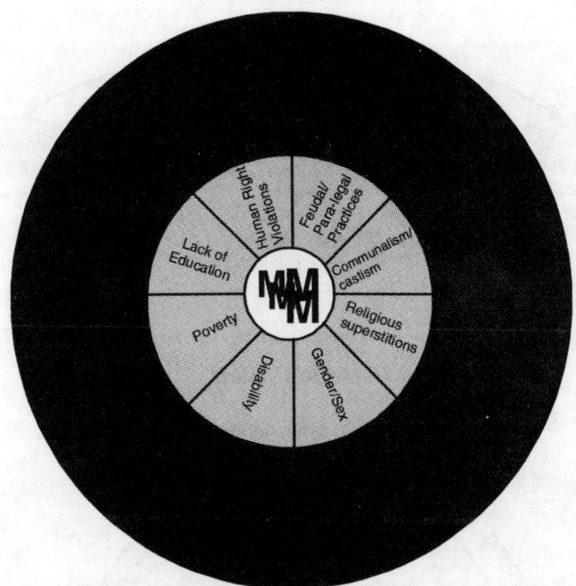

Wheel and Cycle

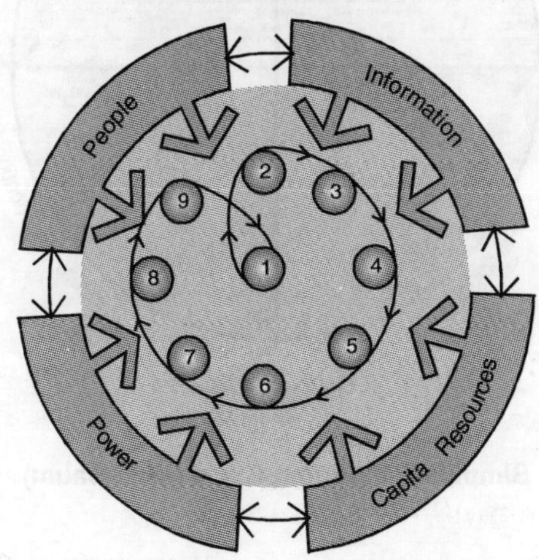

Governance Cycle is the Integration of People, Power, Capital Resources and Information

Interlinked Ellipses

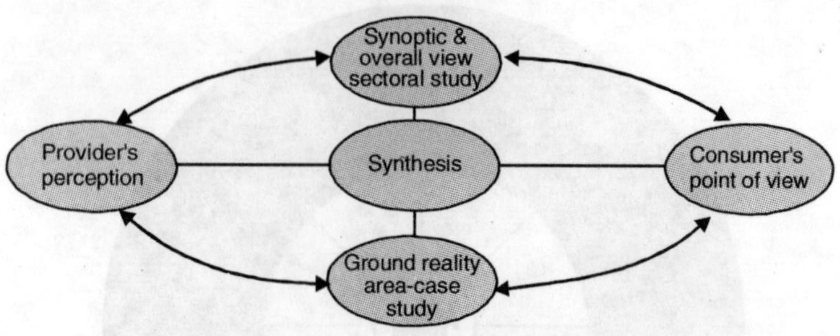

Rotating Wheel

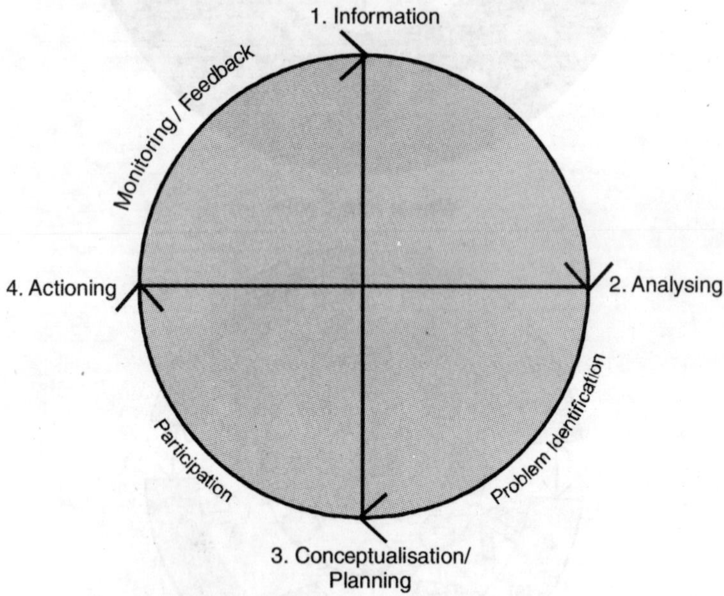

Simplified Planning Cycle (after Baum)

Networked Spheres

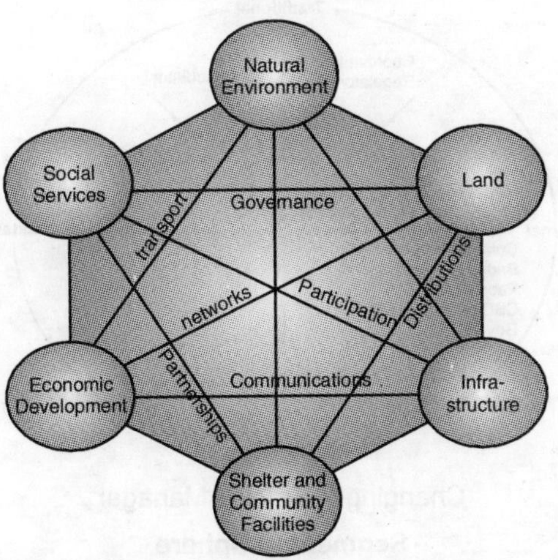

Segmented Sphere

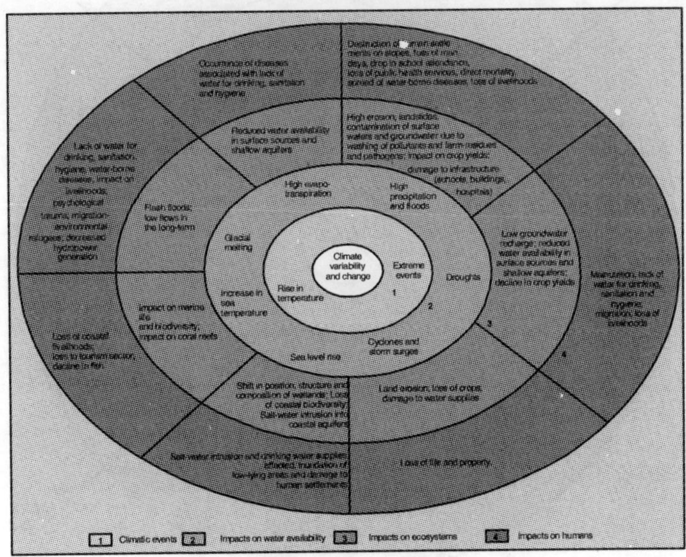

Impact of climate change on Ecology

Wheel and Spokes

Changing Role of a Manager

Segmented Sphere

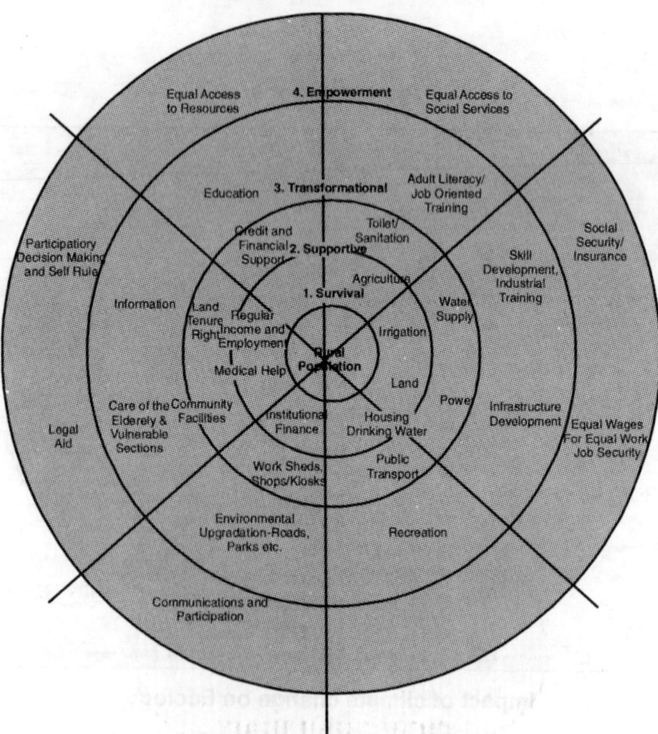

Diagrammatic Classification of the Needs of the Poor

Hexagon and Circles

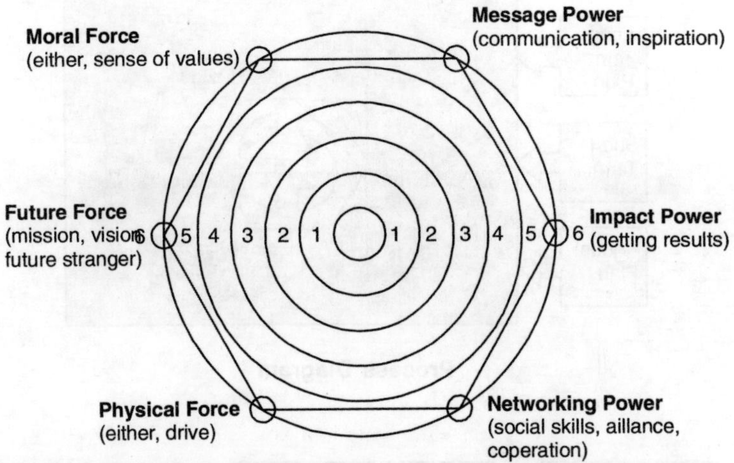

Interlocking Bubbles and Balloons

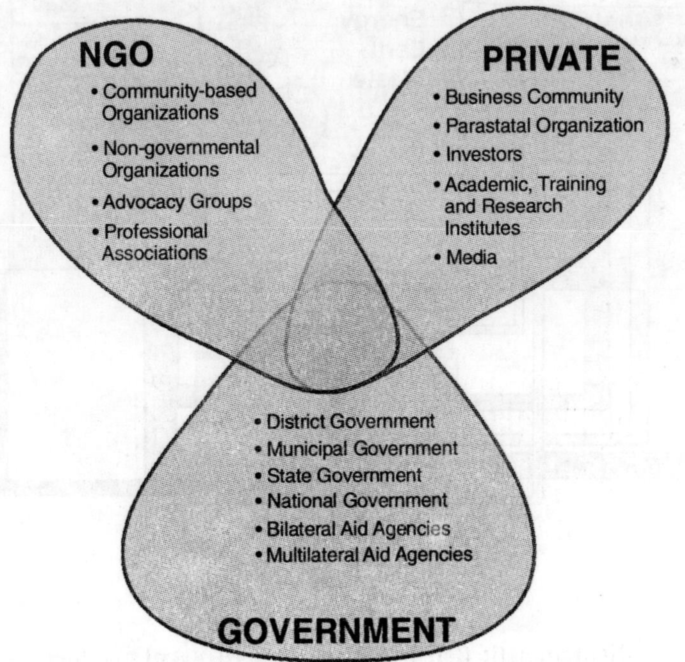

Process Diagram

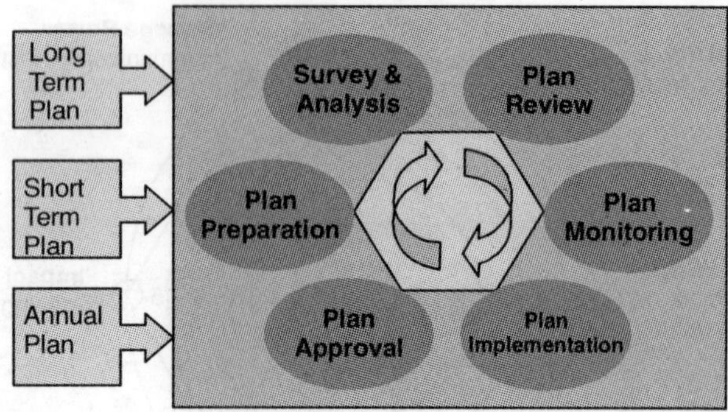

Process Diagram

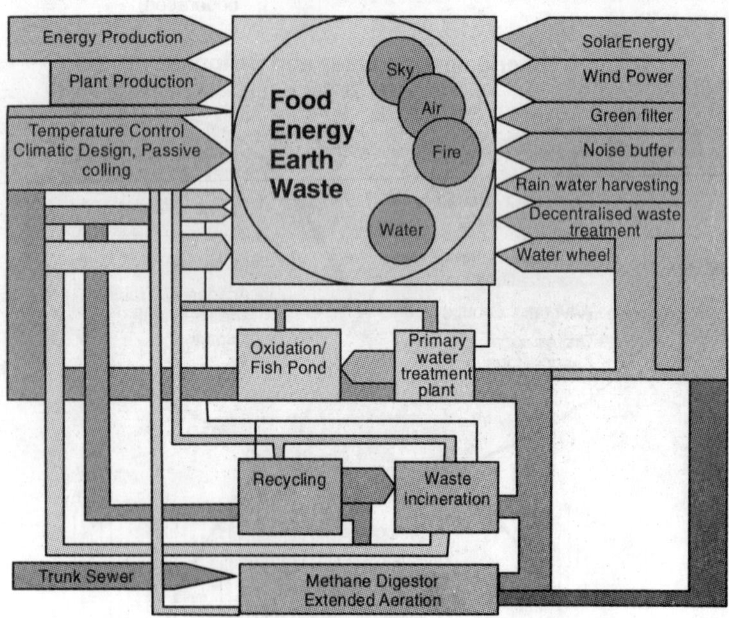

Process Chart

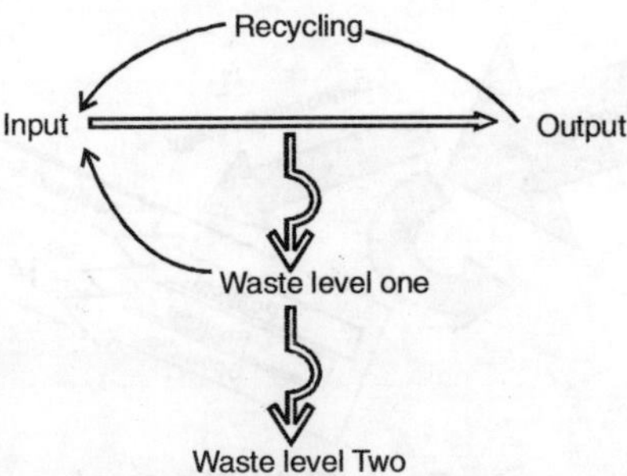

Interlinked Boxes and Triangles

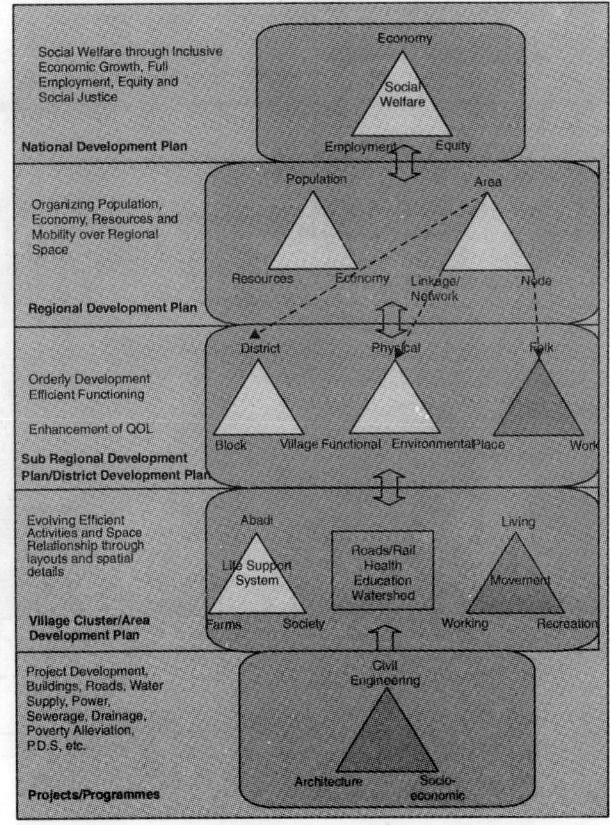

Inter-linkage between Development, Planning and Projects

Arrow Chart

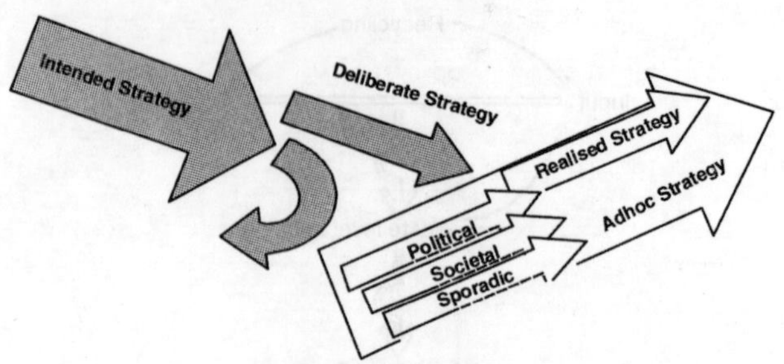

Force Field Chart

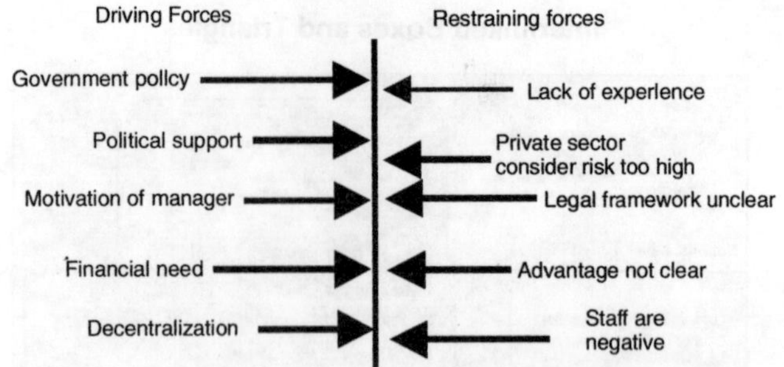

Process Diagram

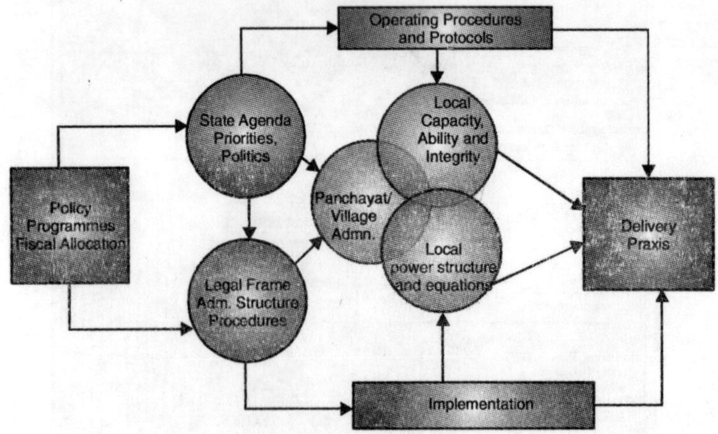

Ladder Diagram

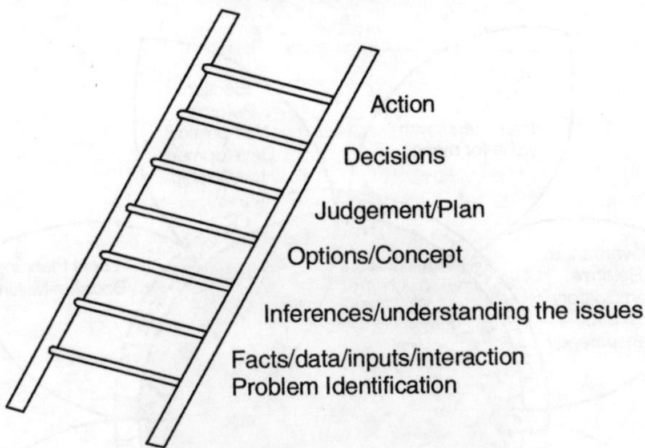

Flow Diagram

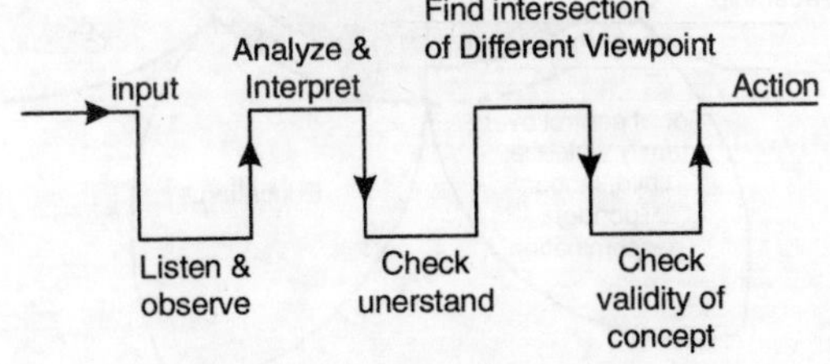

Sun Diagram

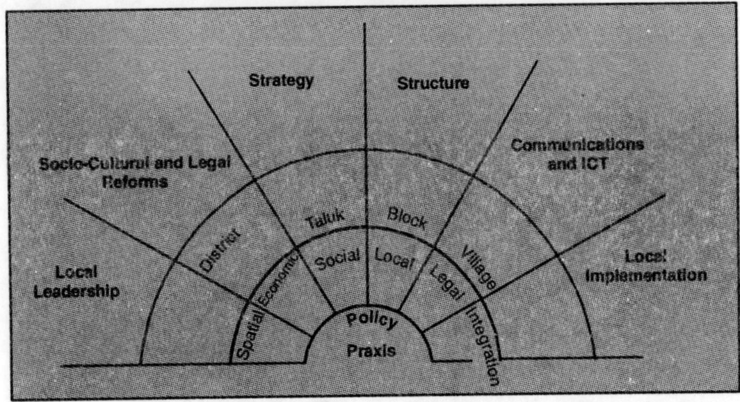

Flower Chart

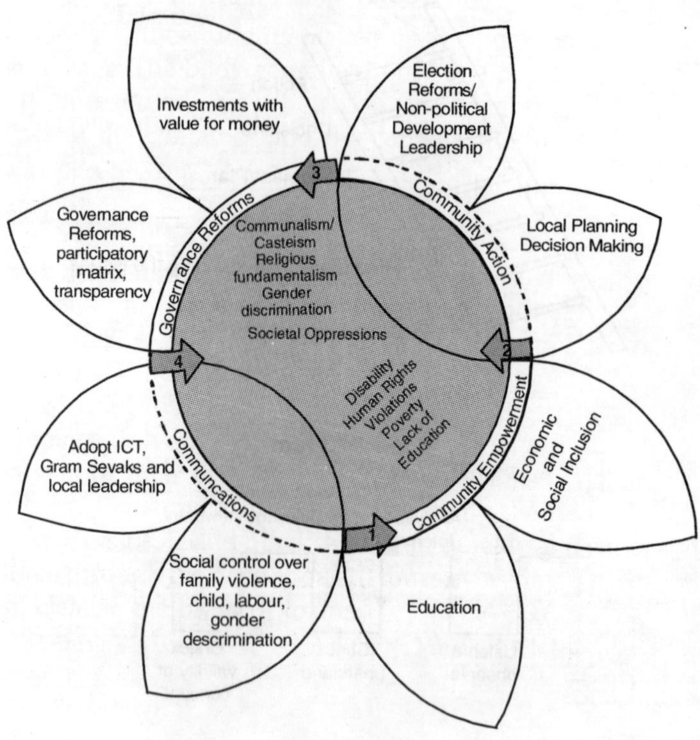

Cloud Envelope

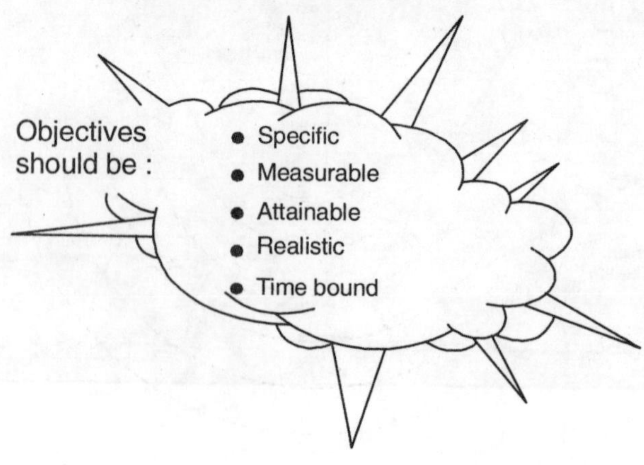

Polygon Chart

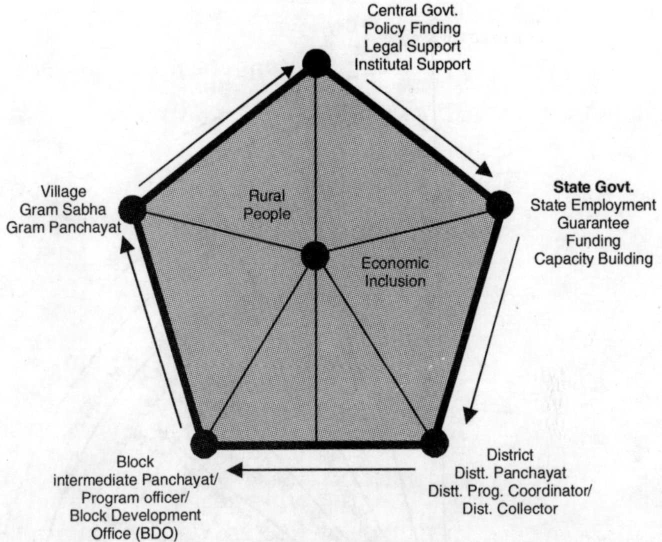

Spiral Chart

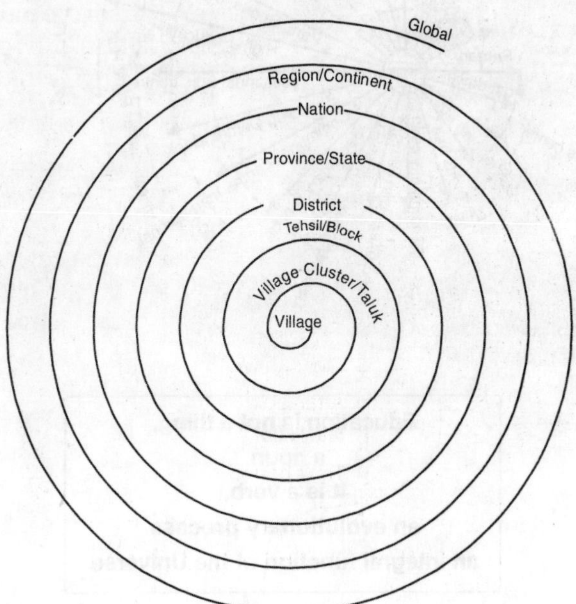

An Evolving Shell Chart

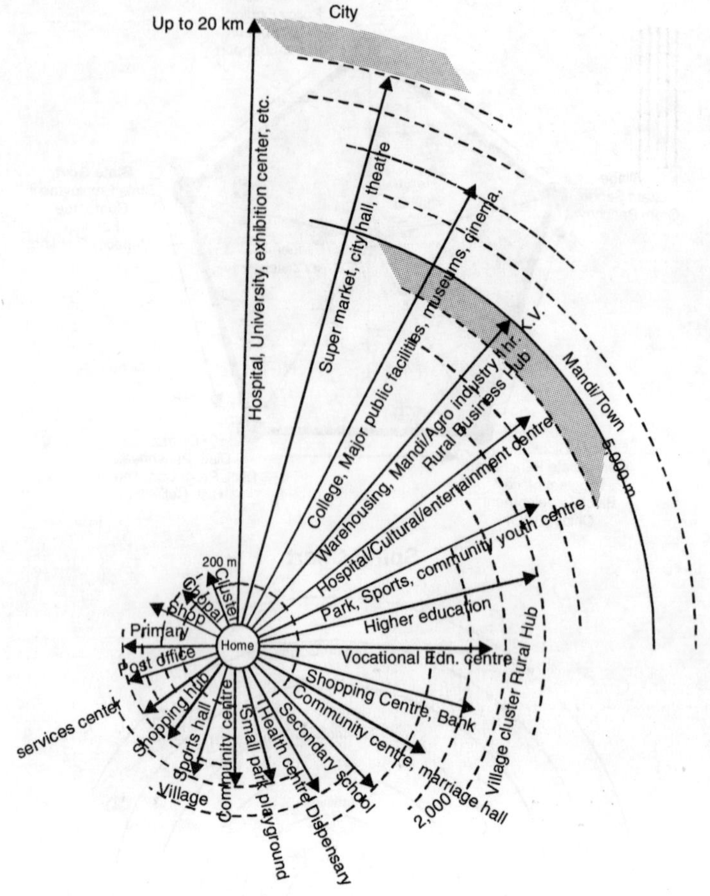

Education is not a thing,
a noun.
It is a verb,
an evolutionary process
an integral function of the Universe

Interlinked Wheels and Chain

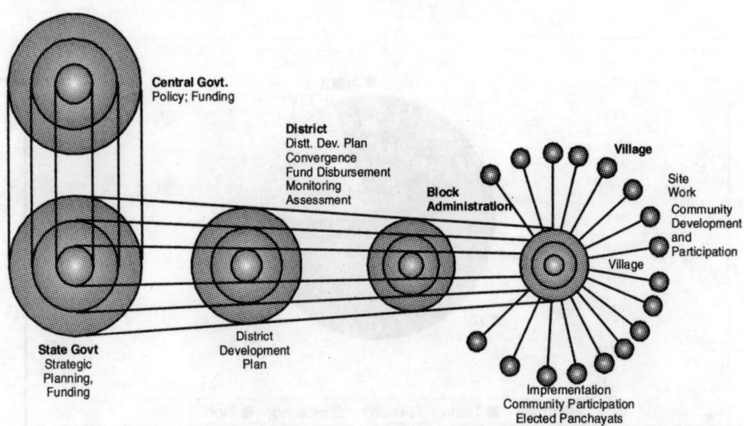

CARTOONS

The extent paper work in inversely proportional to transparency and delivery.

Among various forms of communication, sight delivers about 75 per cent of information

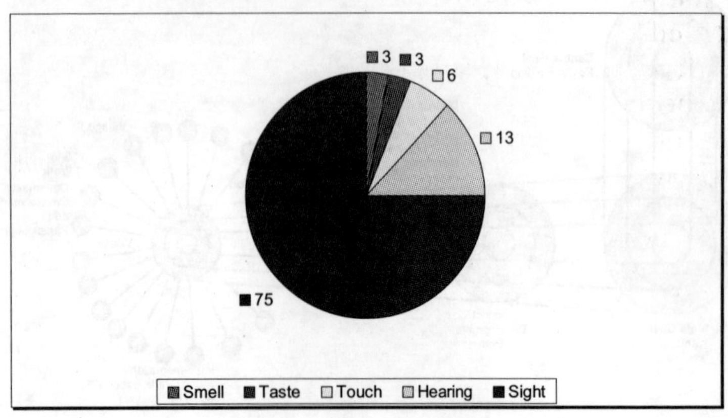

A picture tells thousand words. It helps to create interest among listeners and to hold their attention. Difficult concepts which are critical for understanding of the topic can be explained more clearly with the help of the visuals. Visuals also help to illustrate the linkages, relationships and concepts. These also facilitate a wider spread of the presentations though internet and can be stored for future reference.

Visual aids should be simple and contextual. Pictures and diagrams should be clear and accurate. Colour can be used to highlight the major points and differences. Oral explanation of the visual should be brief and complement the visual. The visual should avoid long text and captions, and even if it is necessary, should not be read out word by word. Participants interaction and questions help in better understanding of the subject. Structure should have a consistent storyline and gradual transition from known to unknown, from simple to complex, from observation to analysis, from analysis to abstractions and from general to particular.

It is befitting to end the book quoting Dr. Ashok K. Chauhan, who in his foreword writes : "We have long way to go. We always remember that university education is the most important segment of nation building and its future. As such, we have to give our best to society and nation, not just for the present, but for posterity. While gratified by the fulfilled vision of making one of the most remarkable contribution to higher learning, I always remember the words of Robet Frost *"The woods are lovely, dark and deep, But I have promises to keep, And miles to go before I sleep, And miles to go before I sleep"*.

most important segment of nation building and its future. As such, we have to give our best to society and nation, not just for the present, but for posterity. While gratified by the fulfilled vision of making one of the most remarkable contribution to higher learning, I always remember the words of Robert Frost: "The woods are lovely, dark and deep, But I have promises to keep, And miles to go before I sleep, And miles to go before I sleep".

References

Beyer, B.K. 1987. Practical strategies for the teaching of thinking. Boston: Allyn & Bacon.

Bono Edward de, 1970, Lateral Thinking, Penguin Books, London.

Browne, M.N., and S.M. Keeley. 1986. Asking the right questions: A guide to critical thinking. 2d ed. Englewood Cliffs, New Jersey : Prentice-Hall.

Ernest and Young and FICCI 2010 High Education : Expansion and Excellence, Vision 2025, New Delhi.

Jadhav, Dr. Narendra, 2010 a must for growth of ITIs and Polytechnics, Digital Learning (May).

Jain A.K., 2012, Towards Excellence in Technical Education in India, 1BC News, New Delhi.

Jain A.K., 2013, Dream, Think, Design, Address in National Assn. of Students of Architecture, Dasna (UP).

Jain A.K., 2013, Curriculum Reforms in Town and Country Planning Education, ITPI, AICTE National Colloquium, New Delhi.

Mantha S.S., June, 2012, Technical Education in the New World Order, in Digital Learning.

Pearson Education, June, 2012, Bringing about the Learning Revolution, in Digital Learning.

Rawllinson, J.G., Creative Thinking and Brainstorming, Gohar, London

Shiba, Shoji and David Wallace, 1993, Four Practical Revolutions in Management, Centre for Quality of Management, Cambridge, Massachusetts

Shaw, George Bernard., 1903. Man and superman: A comedy and a philosophy. In Dan H. Laurene (Ed.) *Bernard Shaw: Collected Plays with their Prefaces*, Vol. 2. (London: Max Reinhardt, The Badley Head), 1971.

Thiek, L. Paul, Indra's Net and the Midas touch: Living sustainably in a connected world. The MIT Press, Cambridge, MA, 2011.

Tuckman, B.W. (1965). "Developmental Sequence in Small Groups", *Psychological Bulletin 63:* 384-399. The article was reprinted in *Group Facilitation: A Research and Applications Journal 3,* Spring 2001.

UN, 1948, The Universal Declaration of Human rights. http://www.un.org/en/documents/udhr/index.shtml

UNESCOTowards Knowledge Societies United National Educational, Scientific and Cultural Oranisation Paris, 2005, http//www.unesco.org/publications

UNICEF (1996). *Education for Conflict Resolution : A Training Manual*. New York and Geneva.

———— (1996). *Games and Exercises: A Manual for Facilitation and Trainers Involved in Participatory Group Events, New York.*

www.planningcommission.nic.in
www.digitallearning.in

Index

A

Absorbed and provoked, 81

Adam, 40

All India Council for Technical Education (AICTE), 1, 3

Anonymous, 78

Ashtanga yoga, 20

B

Bell, Alexander Graham, 32

Bhagavad Gita, 29

Bhirthrihari, 16
- in Shatakatrayi, 41

Buddha (Gautama), 34

Buzz sessions, 44

C

Celibacy and simplicity, 17

Chair, 45

Chaos, 40

Chhandogya Upanishad, 21

Chinmayananda, Swami, 28

Collier, Robert, 73

Communicating effectively, 78-105
- among various forms of communication, sight delivers about 75 per cent of information, 104
- be clear, 80-81
- graphic tools, 81-105
- interlinked boxes and triangles, 97
- polygon chart, 101
- rating of key components in development delivery, 90
- stepped matrix chart, 85
- sun diagram, 99
- various types of graphics, 83

Concentration and Mediation, 22

Culture of excellence and performance, 29

D

Digital literacy, 68

Dodson, Fitzhugh, 37

Drishti, 21

E

Education-Industry Interface, 7

Einstein, Albert, 35, 74

F

Faculty Orientation, 7

Finisher, 45

Franklin, Benjamin, 42

Frost, Robert, 105

G

Gandhi (Mahatma), 1, 34

Gate keeping, 51

Gates, Pearly, 40
GDP, 3
Graham, Martha, 58
Guru Drona, 22
Gyan, 22

H

Hamilton, Brutus, 33

I

IBMT, 20
ICT, 62, 67
Idea of learning, 13-40
- active learning, 35-37
- Barm cycle of learning, 15-17
- barriers to learning, 14
- cleansing, decluttering and unlearning, 16
- enlarging understanding, 30-32
- focus, 25-26
- listening and learning, 28-29
- meditation improves brain wiring, 20-25
- multiview, 26-27
- rigour, dogged persistence, 32-34
- soft and hard mediums, 37-40
- values, 34-35
- we wash and purify our body everyday, but often forget to cleanse our mind, 17-20

IIMs, 37
India Against Corruption, 65
Individual skills, 46
Innovation, 62
Innovator, 45
INSEAD, 37
IT, 17

K

Kabir, 29
Kalam, A.P.J. Abdul, 12

L

Learning Management System (LMS), 63
Ling, Lee W., 34

M

Maharshi, Ramana, 61
Master, Zen, 30
Metaphysicians, 34
Ministry of Human Resource Development, 1
MIT Lincoln Laboratory, 60

N

Newton, 55
NGOs, 3

O

Obama, Barack, 65
OELE, 63, 64
Open Technology Platform, 63
Oral explanation, 104
Organizational learning, 57
Orientation programmes, 4
Overseas Development Institute, 72

P

Participatory learning, 41-55
- communication, 48
- content versus process, 47-48
- decision-making procedure, 48-49
- emotional issues, 51-54
- group behaviour, 45-47

individual characteristics, 54-55

chair, 54

evaluator, 55

finisher, 55

innovator, 54

organiser, 55

resource investigator, 54

shaper, 54

team worker, 55

rules of participatory learning, 44-45

self-oriented behaviour, 50

types of behaviour relevant to group learning, 50-51

Patanjali, 20

Path of realization of success by learning, 13

PC, 63

Personal Action Plan, 76

Personal organisation, 73-77

education or learning, 74-77

Pranayam, 20

Problem solving, 68

Professional education in India, 1-12

changing roles, 12

education and industry interface, 7-9

rethinking learning and skill development, 9-11

Purchasing Power Parity, 3

Q

QIP, 7

R

Ramakrishna, 19

Resource Investigator, 45, 54

S

Sama Veda, 44

Sanskar, 38

Sanskriti, 21

Second Life, 66

Seeking decision, 50

Shakespeare, William, 6

Shaper, 45

Shvetaketu, 21

SMART, 65

Standard setting and testing, 51

Synergy of group thinking, action and behaviour, 42

T

Team Worker, 45

Types of behaviour, 52

U

U.S. Olympic Sailing Team, 25

UCLA, 76

UNICEF, 71, 72

Universal Self, 20

University Grants Commission, 1

V

Vivekananda, Swami, 13, 56

W

Williams, Monier, 21

World Bank, 1

World War II, 37

World-class education, 56-72

embedded learning, 61-62

improvised performance, 58

inspiration from masters, 59

Intel model for education transformation, 66-69

lateral thinking, 69-72
blue hat, 71-72
green hat, 70
grey hat, 70
red hat, 71
white hat, 69-70
yellow hat, 70-71
mastering a skill, 59
myth of talent and luck, 59-61
new generation technology, 62-63
social learning, 65-66
social media for learning, 67
technology platforms and open ended learning, 63-65

Y

Yoga, 20
Yoga gurus, 20